Weird Facts for Adults
This Really Happened - History's Strangest Mysteries and Unbelievable True Stories

Les Brady

Medialusion Books

Contents

Introduction

I N A WORLD WHERE history is often reduced to dry dates and sterile facts, there are stories so bizarre, so utterly fantastic, that they seem to defy explanation. Yet these tales aren't pulled from the pages of fiction, they're real events that shaped our world in unexpected ways.

Imagine a city where people danced themselves to death, a morning when meat literally rained from the sky, or a time when an entire Roman legion vanished only to potentially resurface in ancient China. These aren't plots from alternate history novels, they're documented incidents that challenge our understanding of what's possible.

As we journey through these ten historical mysteries, we'll encounter phenomena that would seem outlandish even in fiction: a devastating flood of molasses that reshaped industrial safety standards, mysterious footprints that traversed 100 miles of Victorian England in a single night, and a group of brave government workers who voluntarily ate poison to protect future generations.

But these stories are more than just historical curiosities. They're windows into the human experience, revealing how our ancestors faced the inexplicable and how their responses continue to influence our world today. From the mass hysteria that gripped a small Illinois town during World War II to the creative deceptions that helped win that same war, each chapter unveils how truth can indeed be stranger, and more fascinating, than fiction.

So prepare yourself for a journey through some of history's most perplexing moments. These aren't just stories to read, they're conversations waiting to happen, mysteries begging to be discussed, and reminders that history is far more remarkable than we sometimes imagine. Whether you're a history enthusiast, a curious skeptic, or someone who simply loves a good story, these tales will challenge what you think you know about the past.

In the pages that follow, we'll explore events that have baffled experts, challenged scientific explanation, and left lasting marks on human society. We'll examine the evidence, consider the theories, and ultimately confront a humbling truth: that sometimes the most unbelievable stories are the ones that actually happened.

Chapter 1

The Dancing Plague of 1518

When a City Couldn't Stop Moving

I N THE SWELTERING SUMMER of 1518, the streets of Strasbourg witnessed one of history's most peculiar epidemics, not of fever, plague, or any known disease, but of dancing. What began with a lone woman dancing feverishly in the marketplace would soon spiral into a crisis that would grip the city for more than a month, leaving authorities scrambling for answers and hundreds of citizens literally dancing themselves to exhaustion. Fear gripped the city as more and more people joined this bizarre spectacle, their bodies moving uncontrollably in a macabre dance that would last for days on end. Picture this, you're a medieval city guard, standing watch over Strasbourg's marketplace when suddenly you notice someone dancing. No big deal, right? Except they're not stopping. Hours pass, and they're still going. Then others join in, not by choice, but as if possessed by some invisible force that commands their bodies to move.

I've seen some weird things in my travels across America's backroads, giant balls of twine, houses made of bottles, even a museum dedicated to banana peels, but nothing quite compares to what happened in Strasbourg that summer. Before long, scholars estimate around 400 people were caught in this dancing frenzy. And I don't mean they were having some medieval version of a dance party. We're talking about people dancing until their feet were bloody, their bodies exhausted, and some literally danced themselves to death.

The local authorities, bless their medieval hearts, had absolutely no idea what to do. Their solution? In what has to be one of history's most questionable medical decisions, they decided that the best way to cure this dancing fever was... wait for it... more dancing! They actually built stages and hired musicians to play for the affected people. It's like trying to cure a coffee addiction by opening an espresso stand in someone's living room.

Here's where it gets really interesting, this wasn't happening in some superstitious dark age where people thought the moon was made of cheese. This was 1518, when Strasbourg was a bustling, sophisticated city. We have detailed medical records, official documents, and firsthand accounts of the whole bizarre affair. The victims weren't just making this up, they were experiencing something very real and terrifying.

Modern scientists have tried to explain it as mass hysteria triggered by the perfect storm of circumstances, extreme heat, food shortages, and social tension. But honestly? I've spent enough time digging through historical records to know that sometimes the more we explain something, the more mysterious it becomes. Think about it, we live in a world where people can't even keep their New Year's resolution to go to the gym twice a week, yet these folks danced non-stop for days. It wasn't just impressive; it was impossible. Yet it happened.

What makes this story even more fascinating is how it messes with our modern assumptions about mass behavior. We like to think we're too sophisticated now for something like this to happen. But guess what? Cases of mass psychogenic illness still pop up today, they just look different. Instead of dancing, we might see waves of mysterious symptoms spreading through social media. The human mind, it turns out, hasn't changed as much as we'd like to think.

As we dig deeper into this fascinating piece of history, we'll explore not just what happened, but why it matters to us today. After all, if there's one thing I've learned from chasing down historical oddities across the country, it's that the strangest stories often tell us the most about who we are as human beings.

The Outbreak: From One Dancer to Mass Hysteria

You know that feeling when you're at a wedding and someone starts the "YMCA" and suddenly everyone's compelled to do those arm movements? Well, multiply that by about a thousand, add some medieval panic, and you're getting close to what happened in Strasbourg. Let me paint you a picture of how this whole bizarre episode kicked off.

It started with Frau Troffea[1][4], who stepped into the streets one scorching July day and began to dance. Now, I'm not talking about a quick jig or a celebratory twirl, this was full-on, non-stop movement that went on for days. No music, no rhythm, just pure, relentless dancing. The locals probably thought she'd had a bit too much ale at first, but as the hours turned into days, it became clear something far stranger was afoot.

Within a week, thirty other people had joined this involuntary dance party[1]. By month's end, Strasbourg had transformed into what I can only describe as history's most tragic flash mob, up to 400 people gyrating, spinning, and leaping through the streets[1][2][4]. It wasn't fun or festive; these folks were in serious distress. They danced until their feet were bleeding, their bodies drenched in sweat, some even dropping dead from exhaustion, heart attacks, and strokes[1][2][4].

Now, here's where things get really wild. The city officials, in what has to be one of history's most questionable emergency responses, decided the best way to handle this crisis was to encourage more dancing[1][3]. I kid you not, they built special stages and hired musicians, basically turning a medical emergency into a city-sponsored dance marathon. It's like trying to cure hiccups by giving someone more hiccups.

The victims weren't having a good time, they were screaming for help, their faces twisted in agony as their bodies moved against their will[4]. This bizarre outbreak affected everyone from wealthy merchants to humble peasants, proving that this 'dance fever' didn't discriminate based on social status. The city's guild halls became makeshift hospitals for exhausted dancers, while local physicians scratched their heads and blamed it on 'hot blood', which was basically medieval-speak for 'we have no clue what's happening here.'[3]

But wait, there's more! This wasn't even an isolated incident. Similar outbreaks had been popping up along the Rhine River between the 10th and 16th centuries[3][5]. It's like the region had a recurring case of the medieval dance fever, though none quite matched the scale of Strasbourg's 1518 show.

Modern experts generally chalk this up to mass psychogenic illness[1][2][3][4], basically, when extreme psychological stress hits an entire community at once, causing physical symptoms to spread like wildfire. Think of it as a medieval version of a social media panic, but instead of sharing viral posts, people were sharing... well, viral dance moves.

Here's what fascinates me most, we've got detailed records of this whole thing. Multiple eyewitnesses documented it, city council meetings discussed it, and medical professionals of the time wrote about it. This wasn't some vague legend or campfire story; this actually happened. And while we might have fancy scientific terms to explain it now, I'd argue it's still just as mysterious and unsettling as it was five centuries ago.

The dancing finally fizzled out in early September 1518, but let me tell you, Strasbourg was never quite the same after that. I mean, how could it be? When you've seen your neighbors literally dance themselves to death, it tends to leave an impression.

Medical and Social Responses in Medieval Strasbourg

Let me tell you about medieval medicine's greatest hits, and by hits, I mean complete misses. Picture yourself as Strasbourg's top doctor in 1518. Folks are dancing themselves to death in the streets, and you've got to come up with a solution fast. What's your brilliant medical advice? "Dance it out!"[4] Yeah, you read that right.

See, these medieval physicians had this wild theory about "hot blood", kind of like how my Uncle Pete explains away all his problems as "that's just how it is." They figured the only way to cure this dancing fever was to let people boogie until they couldn't boogie anymore[4]. It's like treating a hangover with more alcohol, sounds fun in theory, terrible in practice.

The city officials, bless their medieval hearts, went all in on this idea. They transformed Strasbourg into what I can only describe as history's deadliest dance festival. They built stages throughout the city, hired musicians (talk about job security!), and even brought in professional dancers to "help" the afflicted[6]. Imagine being one of those professional dancers, worst gig ever.

Now, you might be wondering, "How did nobody realize this was a terrible idea?" Well, context is everything. Strasbourg was already dealing with a buffet of problems, famine, disease outbreaks, and social unrest[3]. People were stressed out of their minds, which modern experts say created perfect conditions for mass psychogenic illness[6]. Think of it as medieval Twitter, one person posts something dramatic, and suddenly everyone's caught up in the chaos.

The physical toll was devastating. People weren't just dancing, they were destroying themselves. We're talking bloodied feet, swollen limbs, and faces twisted in agony[2]. Some victims would cry out for help while their bodies kept moving against their will. The death toll? Reports suggest up to 15 people were dying each day at the peak of this crisis[2].

When the "dance it out" strategy predictably failed (shocker!), the city switched to Plan B, religion. They started carting dancers off to shrines dedicated to Saint Vitus, the patron saint of dancers and epilepsy[2]. I've seen some desperate Hail Mary passes in my roadside adventures across America, but this one takes the medieval cake.

Here's what gets me, while we might laugh at their "solutions" now, these medieval folks were genuinely trying their best with what they knew. They documented everything meticulously, conducted what they considered scientific observations, and genuinely tried to help (even if their help made things worse). It's like watching someone try to fix their computer by talking sweetly to it, the intention is pure, even if the method is questionable.

But perhaps the most fascinating part? This whole episode fundamentally changed how Strasbourg's society viewed collective behavior and medical treatment. It's like they had their own version of a public health wake-up call, medieval style. Sure, they got it completely wrong, but at least they were paying attention.

Looking back, the Dancing Plague of 1518 teaches us something important about human nature, sometimes our attempts to help can make things worse, especially when we're working with incomplete information. It's a humbling reminder that even with the best intentions, we might still be the equivalent of medieval doctors prescribing more dancing to cure a dancing plague. Makes you wonder what future generations will think about some of our "obvious" solutions, doesn't it?

Theories and Historical Impact of the Dancing Plague

You know what really bakes my noodle about the Dancing Plague? The more we try to explain it, the weirder it gets. I've spent countless hours in dusty archives and spoken with every expert who'd give me the time of day, and let me tell you, this rabbit hole goes deep.

Let's start with the ergot theory, since it's everyone's favorite medieval party crasher. Some folks suggested the dancers had eaten grain contaminated with ergot, a fungus that's chemically similar to LSD[17]. Sounds plausible, right? Except ergot poisoning typically turns you into a human puddle, not a dancing machine[7]. Trust me, I've seen what ergot does to grain during my travels through farming communities, it's more "help, I can't move" than "hey, let's boogie!"

The theory that makes the most sense comes from historian John Waller, who argues this was a case of mass psychogenic illness, what we used to call mass hysteria[327]. Now, before you roll your eyes at the 'hysteria' explanation, consider what Strasbourg was dealing with in 1518. The city was basically experiencing a medieval version of Murphy's Law, everything that could go wrong, did go wrong.

We're talking devastating famines that made modern food shortages look like a minor inconvenience. Grain prices had shot through the roof[37]. Diseases were running rampant, smallpox, syphilis, you name it[3]. As Waller puts it (and I love this quote): "Even by the grueling standards of the Middle Ages, these were bitterly harsh years for the people of Alsace."[7]

Here's where it gets really interesting, the locals believed in something called the curse of St. Vitus. According to this belief, if you ticked off this particular saint, he might force you to dance until you dropped[37]. It's like having a divine DJ who won't let you leave the dance floor. This belief created what psychologists call a 'behavioral script', basically, it gave people's anxiety a specific way to manifest.

But here's what I find absolutely mind-blowing: this wasn't just some isolated medieval meltdown. Similar dance outbreaks kept popping up along the Rhine River between the 10th and 16th centuries[3]. It's like the region had a recurring case of dance fever, though none quite matched Strasbourg's epic performance.

The 1518 incident stands out because it's the most well-documented case of dancing mania in European history[3]. We've got everything from medical records to city council minutes. It's become the historical equivalent of a case study in how stress, cultural beliefs, and social pressure can make people do some truly extraordinary things.

And let me tell you something really wild, we're not as different from those medieval dancers as we might think. Mass psychogenic illness still happens today; it just looks different. Instead of dancing, modern outbreaks might involve mysterious symptoms spreading through social media or unexplained illnesses in schools or workplaces. The human mind hasn't changed much in 500 years, we're just as capable of being influenced by collective beliefs and fears.

What fascinates me most about the Dancing Plague isn't just what happened, but what it reveals about human nature. Under the right conditions, our minds can make our bodies do things that seem impossible. These people danced for days despite exhaustion, injury, and even death. It's a reminder that the line between mind and body isn't as clear as we like to think.

The legacy of the Dancing Plague lives on in more than just history books. It's shaped our understanding of mass psychology, influenced studies in collective behavior, and reminded us that sometimes the most unbelievable stories are the ones that actually happened. Next time you're at a wedding and the DJ won't stop playing the Chicken Dance, just be thankful it's only for one song, not one month. You know what keeps me up at night about the Dancing Plague of 1518? Not just the bizarre spectacle of hundreds of people dancing themselves to exhaustion, though that's plenty disturbing. What really gets me is how this whole incident challenges everything we think we know about human behavior and collective psychology.

I've seen some strange things in my travels, ghost towns where people swear the tumbleweeds dance at midnight, diners where the pie is so good it should be illegal, but nothing quite compares to what happened in Strasbourg that summer. We're not talking about a few people cutting loose at a festival here. We're talking about hundreds of ordinary folks dancing until their feet bled, their bodies gave out, and in some tragic cases, until their hearts literally stopped beating.

The truly mind-bending part? We have solid historical documentation of the whole thing. This isn't some folktale that got exaggerated over centuries of retellings. We've got medical records, city council minutes, and eyewitness accounts from reliable sources. It's like having HD footage of Bigfoot, except this actually happened.

Modern science tells us this was probably mass psychogenic illness, triggered by a perfect storm of social stress, religious beliefs, and dire living conditions. But you know what? That explanation, while technically accurate, feels about as satisfying as calling Beethoven's Ninth Symphony "just some notes arranged in a particular order." It doesn't quite capture the profound mystery of how hundreds of human minds and bodies could synchronize in such a devastating dance.

What really strikes me is how this event exposes the razor-thin line between order and chaos in human society. One minute you're going about your medieval business, maybe haggling over the price of turnips in the market square, and the next thing you know, you're caught in an unstoppable dancing frenzy. It reminds us that even today, we're not as far removed from such collective behaviors as we might think, we just express them differently.

So the next time someone tells you that history is boring, or that we modern folks are too sophisticated for mass hysteria, remind them about the Dancing Plague of 1518. Tell them about Frau Troffea, who stepped into the streets one summer day and sparked one of history's most bizarre epidemics. Sometimes the strangest stories are the ones that actually happened, and sometimes the most important lessons about human nature come from the moments when society started dancing and couldn't stop.

Chapter 2

The Great Molasses Flood

Boston's Strangest Disaster

O N AN UNUSUALLY WARM winter day in Boston's North End, the air carried an overwhelming sweet scent that would soon turn sinister. What started as a typical January afternoon in 1919 would become one of history's most peculiar industrial disasters, proving that sometimes the most innocent of substances can become deadly weapons. The viscous brown wave that engulfed Boston's North End that fateful day became one of America's most bizarre cautionary tales, proving that even the sweetest substances can turn deadly under the right circumstances.

Imagine 2.3 million gallons of molasses, enough to fill an Olympic swimming pool one and a half times over, suddenly breaking free from its steel prison. The tank's collapse wasn't just a simple leak; it was a catastrophic failure that sent a sticky tsunami through the streets at 35 miles per hour. That's faster than most people can run, which is exactly why so many couldn't escape its path. The wave was strong enough to lift a train right off its tracks and bend steel girders like they were made of taffy.

But here's the really wild part, the disaster was practically a perfect storm of physics gone wrong. That unusually warm January day (a positively balmy 40 degrees Fahrenheit) caused the molasses to heat up and get all excited at the molecular level. Anyone who's ever tried to pour warm molasses knows it moves a lot faster than the cold stuff. Now imagine that effect multiplied by about a million, add in some questionable construction standards from the 1910s, and you've got yourself a recipe for the strangest disaster in American history.

The aftermath was like something out of a bizarre fever dream. Picture firefighters and rescue workers wading through waist-deep molasses, trying to save people while getting progressively stickier. The clean-up took weeks, and they say that on hot summer days, you could still smell molasses in Boston's North End for decades afterward. Some old-timers swear they can catch a whiff of it even today.

But this wasn't just a sticky situation, it was a wake-up call for industrial safety in America. Before the Great Molasses Flood, companies could pretty much build whatever they wanted, however they wanted. After 21 people lost their lives to a wave of sweetener, suddenly everyone got real interested in things like structural engineering and building codes. Who knew it would take a molasses tsunami to revolutionize industrial safety regulations?

The Physics of Disaster: How Temperature and Poor Construction Created a Perfect Storm

Ever wonder why molasses is so sluggish in winter but flows like syrup in summer? Well, that quirk of physics played a starring role in one of history's strangest disasters. Picture this: a massive steel tank filled with 2.3 million gallons of industrial molasses, that's about 40% heavier than water, by the way[8]. The tank itself was a monument to corner-cutting, with walls so thin they practically flexed in the breeze.

Now, here's where things get scientifically bizarre. In the days leading up to January 15, Boston was experiencing an unseasonable warm spell. Remember how molasses gets all runny when it's warm? That's because heat gives those sticky molecules extra energy to slip and slide past each other. The company had just topped off the tank with a fresh delivery of warm molasses[8 10], creating a perfect storm of physics gone wrong.

The tank's construction was about as sturdy as a house of cards in a hurricane. The steel walls were paper-thin by industrial standards, held together by subpar rivets that were already showing signs of stress. And get this, when the tank started leaking (because of course it did), the brilliant solution was to paint it brown to hide the seepage[8]. Talk about putting lipstick on an industrial disaster pig!

When the tank finally gave way, it unleashed physics at its most terrifying. All that stored potential energy, imagine a building-sized water balloon suddenly popping, converted instantly into kinetic energy. The result? A 25-foot-high wave of molasses moving at 35 miles per hour[8]. That's right, the substance famous for moving slower than, well, molasses, was briefly outpacing Olympic sprinters.

But Mother Nature wasn't done playing her cruel physics jokes. Remember that warm spell? Well, it decided to end right after the flood. The rapidly cooling temperature caused the molasses to thicken quickly[8], turning rescue efforts into a sticky nightmare. Modern scientists like Nicole Sharp are still studying this disaster[9], proving that sometimes the most important physics lessons come from the most unlikely places.

The whole catastrophe reads like a perfect example of Murphy's Law meets fluid dynamics. The density of the molasses, its temperature-dependent viscosity, and structural failure created a disaster that would seem far-fetched even in a Hollywood movie[8 9 10]. It's a stark reminder that the laws of physics don't care whether you're dealing with water, molasses, or anything else, when things go wrong, they go wrong spectacularly.

Sticky Aftermath: The Community Impact and Rescue Efforts

Picture wading through a sea of molasses that's actively trying to pull you under. That's exactly what Boston's first responders faced on that fateful January day. The sticky wave didn't just flow through the streets, it created a bizarre disaster zone where every step could trap you like prehistoric amber[13]. Rescuers found themselves in a surreal situation where their boots would get stuck, their clothes would become hopelessly gummed up, and even their rescue equipment turned into molasses-covered paperweights.

The cleanup effort looked like something from a twisted candy maker's nightmare. Regular water just laughed at the sticky mess, it took saltwater from Boston Harbor, pumped by determined fireboats, to finally start dissolving the stubborn syrup[11]. The scene was so bizarre that one rescue worker reportedly quipped, "This ain't your grandma's pancake topping anymore."

The human toll was devastating, 21 lives lost and 150 injured[11][13][15]. Young Pasquale Iantosca and Maria Distasio, both just 10 years old, had been playing outside enjoying that unusually warm day when the wave struck[11]. Fireman George Layhe had just settled into bed at Engine 31's firehouse when the molasses claimed his life[11]. For days, rescuers couldn't even get an accurate count of victims because the sticky residue made searching nearly impossible[13].

Here's a wild fact, people were tracking molasses as far as Cambridge, miles away, thanks to it hitching rides on boots and wagon wheels[11]. The predominantly immigrant North End neighborhood took the hardest hit[14], with property damage that would make modern insurance adjusters faint, we're talking about $100 million in today's money[13].

But sometimes it takes a sticky situation to bring about real change. The Italian immigrant community, who'd often felt voiceless in city matters, used this disaster as a rallying point. Many decided to pursue U.S. citizenship to gain more say in their neighborhood's future[12]. And get this, the legal battle that followed became one of America's first major class-action lawsuits[14][15], basically writing the book on corporate responsibility.

The really mind-bending part? The tank's supervisor had zero technical qualifications, and nobody had bothered to properly inspect the structure[13]. One official summed it up perfectly in August 1920: "This disaster proved that cold molasses can be just as deadly as any tornado when it decides to go rogue."[12] Talk about a sticky situation that changed history, this mess led to tougher building codes, mandatory engineering certifications, and industrial safety rules that probably saved countless lives[12 13 15]. Who knew molasses would be the thing that finally got corporate America to clean up its act?

Legal Legacy: How Molasses Changed Industrial Safety Laws

You'd think a sticky mess would lead to equally sticky legal proceedings, but the aftermath of the Great Molasses Flood moved through the courts with surprising speed. What followed was a groundbreaking legal battle that would revolutionize how America handled industrial accidents and corporate responsibility.

United States Industrial Alcohol (USIA) faced an avalanche of 125 lawsuits from victims and their families[12]. Their defense strategy? About as solid as their tank construction, they tried blaming anarchists for sabotaging the structure[16]. This conspiracy theory dissolved faster than warm molasses when investigators discovered the tank's supervisor couldn't even read blueprints[16]. Talk about putting the wrong person in charge of a potential disaster!

The court-appointed auditor, Hugh Ogden, didn't sugar-coat his findings. After hearing three years of testimony from over 1,000 witnesses, he basically wrote the book on what not to do when building industrial storage tanks[16]. His report was like a greatest hits album of corporate corner-cutting, from ignoring stress tests to skipping basic safety inspections.

The real kicker? USIA ended up paying $628,000 in damages, that's over $11 million in today's money[12]. Each victim's family received about $7,000[16], which might not sound like much now, but in 1925 it was enough to make corporate executives choke on their morning coffee. This case became one of the first examples of a company being held financially accountable for its negligence on such a massive scale.

But here's the sweetest part of this bitter tale, the legal aftermath transformed industrial safety laws across America. States started requiring actual licensed engineers to inspect and approve construction projects[16][8]. No more "my cousin's friend knows a guy who built a shed once" approach to industrial engineering. Building codes got tougher, regular inspections became mandatory, and companies had to prove they weren't just winging it when it came to public safety[16].

Chief Justice Wilfred Bolster summed it up perfectly when he scolded that "a public which, with one eye on the tax rate, provides itself with an administrative equipment 50 percent qualified, has no right to complain that it does not get a 100 percent product."[8] In other words, you get what you pay for, especially when it comes to public safety.

Today, where that infamous tank once stood in Boston's North End, you'll find a public park[8]. It's a peaceful spot that gives no hint of the sticky disaster that once occurred there. But the flood's influence still flows through our legal system, proving that sometimes it takes a sweet substance turning sour to make lasting change. Who knew molasses would be the thing that finally got America to take industrial safety seriously? You know what's wild about the Great Molasses Flood? It's not just that it happened, it's that it took something as sweet and slow as molasses to wake America up to the dangers of cutting corners on industrial safety. This wasn't just any old disaster, it was a perfect storm of physics gone wrong, corporate negligence, and one very warm January day that turned Boston's North End into the world's stickiest nightmare.

The flood left more than just a sticky residue on Boston's streets. It fundamentally changed how we think about industrial safety in America. Before this disaster, companies could basically build whatever they wanted, however they wanted, and just cross their fingers nothing would go wrong. But when 2.3 million gallons of molasses decided to go rogue, it became pretty clear that the "she'll be right" approach to industrial construction wasn't cutting it anymore.

Here's the thing about molasses, it's supposed to be the poster child for slowness, right? "Slower than molasses in January" was a common saying. Well, tell that to the 35-mph wave that outran people through Boston's streets that day. It's a stark reminder that even the most harmless-seeming things can turn deadly when physics and negligence team up. The next time someone complains about "excessive" safety regulations, maybe remind them about the day molasses decided to prove that sweet doesn't always mean safe.

Chapter 3

The Devil's Footprints

One Night, 100 Miles of Bizarre Tracks Across Victorian England

O N THE MORNING OF February 8th, 1855, the residents of Devon, England, awakened to find their peaceful countryside transformed into the setting of an inexplicable mystery. Stretching across the snow-covered landscape for over 100 miles were peculiar hoof-shaped prints, each measuring about four inches long and three inches wide, forming a near-perfect line that seemed to defy natural explanation. The tracks left people baffled, appearing to traverse impossible paths, over rooftops, through walls, and across frozen rivers without breaking the snow's surface. You know what's really wild about this whole thing? I stumbled across this story while researching weird weather patterns, and let me tell you, these weren't your average animal tracks in the snow. Think about it, we're talking about prints that looked like they came straight out of a monster movie, but this was real life in proper Victorian England!

Now, here's where it gets really interesting, each footprint was spaced exactly eight inches apart, like whatever made them was using a ruler. These weren't some random animal tracks meandering through the countryside. No, these things marched in an almost perfect straight line, like some otherworldly surveyor was marking property lines. And get this, they didn't just stop at walls or fences like normal tracks would. These bad boys would go right up one side of a 14-foot wall and continue down the other side, as if gravity was just a polite suggestion!

The timing couldn't have been more perfect for a good mystery, Victorian England was shivering through one particularly nasty winter, and a fresh blanket of snow had just fallen across South Devon the night before. When folks woke up on February 8th, they found these bizarre tracks zigzagging through their properties, crossing rivers, and even showing up in places where no living creature should've been able to reach. It was like something out of those penny dreadful novels everyone was reading back then.

As you can imagine, the theories started flying faster than a spooked horse. Some folks blamed escaped kangaroos or exotic birds from traveling menageries (because apparently, Victorian England had a surprising number of those kicking around). Others swore it was all an elaborate prank, though no one could figure out how any prankster could have covered such a massive distance in a single night. And then, of course, you had those who went straight for the supernatural explanation, hence the nickname "The Devil's Footprints" that's stuck around to this day.

The local newspapers had a field day with this one. The Illustrated London News even published detailed sketches of the prints, which is pretty lucky for us modern folks trying to piece together what happened. These weren't just rough doodles either, we're talking about careful illustrations that showed exactly how these prints looked, right down to the last detail. You can almost feel the artist's bewilderment as they tried to make sense of what they were drawing.

I've got to tell you, after spending way too much time researching this mystery, what fascinates me most isn't just the physical evidence, it's how this whole incident captures something unique about human nature. Here you have these proper Victorian folks, living in an age of rapid scientific progress and industrial revolution, suddenly confronted with something that completely defied their understanding of the world. It's a reminder that no matter how advanced we think we are, the universe still has plenty of surprises up its sleeve.

The Physical Evidence and Eyewitness Accounts

Let me tell you about the weird and wild evidence from that snowy morning in Devon, because this isn't your typical mysterious footprint story. I've seen my fair share of strange tracks while road-tripping across America's backroads, but nothing quite compares to what those Victorian folks documented in 1855.

First off, we've got these incredibly precise measurements taken by local naturalists who weren't messing around[17]. Each print was consistently between 1.5 and 2.5 inches across, about the size of a donkey's hoof, if that donkey had learned to walk like a tightrope walker. The spacing between prints was exactly 8.5 inches apart, creating this eerily straight line that would make a military drill sergeant proud[18].

Now, here's where it gets really strange. The vicar of Clyst St George, Henry Thomas Ellacombe (who, by the way, wasn't some attention-seeking sensationalist but a respected member of the community), became our unexpected scientific chronicler[17]. This guy meticulously documented everything, we're talking detailed letters, careful tracings of the prints, and even draft correspondence with *The Illustrated London News*. Talk about dedication to the weird!

But wait, it gets better. These weren't just any old tracks in the snow. These things were doing the impossible[18][19]. Picture this: you're following these prints, and suddenly they go straight up a 14-foot wall, continue across the top without disturbing the snow (which is just showing off, if you ask me), and then pick up again on the other side like gravity took a coffee break. They squeezed through drainpipes barely big enough for your arm and casually strolled through locked gardens like they had a master key to the neighborhood.

In Dawlish, some local tough guys decided to play monster hunters, arming themselves with guns and clubs to track down whatever was making these prints[19]. Spoiler alert: they came back empty-handed but with even more questions. The tracks they followed were scaling vertical surfaces and dancing across rooftops like some Victorian-era parkour champion[18][19]. My favorite report comes from Trewman's Exeter Flying Post, where they described how the prints maintained perfect spacing even after crossing that infamous fourteen-foot wall, as if a wall that size was just a minor inconvenience.

The geography of this thing was mind-boggling. We're not talking about a few scattered prints in someone's backyard, these tracks covered over 100 miles, showing up everywhere from Exmouth to Topsham, across the Exe Estuary to Dawlish and Teignmouth, all the way to Totnes and Torquay. They even made appearances in Dorset and Lincolnshire[17][18]. If this was a hoax, it was the most ambitious and well-coordinated prank in history. If it was an animal, it must have been training for an ultramarathon.

Here's what keeps me up at night about this case, the consistency. These weren't random animal tracks that kind of looked similar. These were identical prints appearing simultaneously across dozens of parishes after that snowfall, all showing the same impossible behavior[18][19]. Modern skeptics might roll their eyes, but when you've got this many reliable witnesses and detailed documentation from respected community members, it's hard to just wave it away as mass hysteria or overactive imaginations.

Scientific Theories and Natural Explanations

You know what's funny about scientists? Even when faced with something completely bonkers, they'll still try to make sense of it. Take Dr. Edward Forbes, this respected London naturalist who probably had better things to do with his time than measure mysterious hoofprints in the snow. But there he was, trudging through Devon's countryside, ruler in hand, muttering to himself about how these prints were "unlike anything he had ever encountered in nature."[20]

Now, I've seen some creative scientific theories in my travels, but the explanations for the Devil's Footprints take the cake. Some folks suggested badgers were responsible, which makes about as much sense as blaming it on tap-dancing squirrels. I mean, sure, badgers are nocturnal and they do leave tracks, but last I checked, they can't climb vertical walls or teleport across rooftops. And don't get me started on the otter theory, have you ever seen an otter leave perfect hoof prints?

Then there were the bird theories. The great bustard got thrown into the mix, probably because someone thought "great" meant it could perform great feats of architectural gymnastics. But here's the thing about birds, they tend to leave, you know, bird tracks. Not neat little hoof prints lined up like they're practicing for a military parade.

My personal favorite has to be the "Unipede" theory, yes, that's actually a thing someone suggested. Apparently, this mythical one-footed creature decided to hop around Devon for a night, leaving pairs of prints just to mess with people. Someone clearly got their cryptozoology wires crossed on that one.

Some of the meteorological explanations weren't much better. Sure, weather can do some weird things, I once saw a tornado pick up a lawn chair and deposit it perfectly upright two blocks away. But even the strangest weather patterns don't usually create perfect hoof-shaped impressions that march in straight lines across the countryside.

The human hoax theory at least sounds plausible until you really think about it. Picture this: someone (or a group of someones) somehow coordinating to cover over 100 miles in a single night, in the 1850s, while carrying whatever device they're using to make the prints. Oh, and they'd need to be part spider-monkey to scale those walls and roofs. I've planned some elaborate road trips in my time, but that's a bit much even for me.

Modern zoologists looking at the evidence today tend to lean toward a "perfect storm" explanation, multiple animals, weird weather conditions, and our human tendency to connect unrelated dots into patterns[19][17]. It's like when you're on a long road trip and start seeing shapes in the clouds, except this time, the whole of Devon was connecting dots in the snow.

But here's what keeps nagging at me: none of these explanations fully account for all the evidence. The spacing, the consistency, the impossible paths, it's like trying to solve a jigsaw puzzle where none of the pieces quite fit. Sometimes the most honest scientific answer is simply admitting that we don't know everything. And maybe that's what makes this mystery so enduring, it reminds us that even in our modern world of satellite imagery and motion sensors, some things still defy explanation.

Social Impact and Victorian Media Response

You know what really gets me about this whole Devil's Footprints business? It's not just the mysterious tracks themselves, it's how the whole thing sent Victorian society into an absolute tizzy. Picture this: you've got these prim and proper Victorians, all caught up in their age of reason and scientific progress, suddenly faced with something that makes absolutely zero sense. Talk about a reality check!

The newspapers, particularly The Illustrated London News, couldn't get enough of it[19]. They were pumping out detailed sketches and breathless accounts faster than a caffeine-fueled journalist on deadline. But here's the really interesting bit, they tried to walk this tightrope between sensational reporting and maintaining their reputation as serious publications. You'd have one article soberly discussing possible scientific explanations, right next to another practically suggesting the Devil himself was doing parkour across Devon's rooftops.

Trewman's Exeter Flying Post really captured the mood when they described the public's response as "an excitement worthy of the dark ages"[19]. And boy, were they right! In Dawlish, you had shopkeepers and traders arming themselves with whatever they could find, guns, clubs, pitchforks, forming these impromptu hunting parties like something out of a penny dreadful novel. Can you imagine the local hardware store owner and the baker teaming up to hunt the Devil?

What fascinates me most is how this whole incident became a kind of Rorschach test for Victorian society. The upper classes mostly tried to maintain a skeptical, scientific approach, while still sneaking peeks at their neighbor's footprints. Meanwhile, rural communities were more openly willing to embrace supernatural explanations, though they were practical enough to keep their shotguns loaded just in case[21].

The story spread like wildfire beyond Devon's borders, sparking debates in London drawing rooms and village pubs alike. Every time someone tried to offer a rational explanation, three more impossible features of the tracks would be reported. The press offered up everything from escaped kangaroos to elaborate hoaxes, but none of these explanations could fully account for what people were seeing[21].

The incident became this perfect storm of Victorian cultural tensions, you had scientific rationalism butting heads with traditional supernatural beliefs, all playing out in the newly powerful mass media. Papers across the country picked up the story, turning a local mystery into a national sensation that had everyone looking over their shoulder (and checking their garden for suspicious footprints).

Fact is, the Devil's Footprints stuck around in people's imagination long after the snow melted. The story got tangled up with other Victorian urban legends like Spring-heeled Jack[22], becoming part of this bigger conversation about what people were willing to believe in an age that prided itself on explaining everything. Even today, mention the Devil's Footprints in Devon, and you'll likely get a knowing look and maybe a new theory about what really happened that February night.

If you ask me, what makes this story so fascinating isn't just the mysterious tracks, it's how it shows us that no matter how sophisticated we think we are, a good mystery can still stop us in our tracks and make us wonder if we really know as much as we think we do. Those Victorians, for all their scientific progress and rational thinking, found themselves just as stumped as we are today. And maybe that's not such a bad thing. You know what keeps me up at night about these Devil's Footprints? It's not the mystery itself, though that's plenty mind-bending. It's how this whole incident perfectly captures that moment when our neat, orderly view of the world collides head-on with something that just doesn't fit.

I've spent countless hours poring over the evidence, from Reverend Ellacombe's meticulous notes to those detailed sketches in The Illustrated London News. And here's the thing, the more you dig into it, the less any single explanation makes sense. Trust me,

I've chased down enough roadside oddities to know when something genuinely defies explanation.

What we're left with is this perfect snapshot of a society grappling with the unknown. You've got your scientific-minded folks doing their best to measure and document everything, your practical villagers loading their shotguns (just in case), and everyone in between trying to make sense of something that, quite frankly, still doesn't make sense today.

Some mysteries you solve by finding the right answer. But others, like these Devil's Footprints, you solve by understanding what they tell us about ourselves. How do we react when faced with something that challenges everything we think we know? Those Victorian folks, with all their scientific progress and rational thinking, found themselves just as stumped as we would be today.

Maybe that's why this story still grabs hold of people and won't let go. It reminds us that no matter how many mysteries we solve, no matter how advanced we become, the world can still surprise us. And honestly? I kind of love that about it.

So next time you're trudging through snow and spot some weird tracks, take a moment to imagine those baffled Devonshire folks back in 1855. Whether it was an elaborate hoax, some bizarre natural phenomenon, or something else entirely, those footprints left an impression that's lasted far longer than any marks in the snow.

Chapter 4

The Kentucky Meat Shower

When the Skies Rained Flesh

O N A CRISP MARCH morning in 1876, the residents of Bath County, Kentucky, witnessed something that would challenge the very limits of believability, it began raining meat from a cloudless sky. The chunks of flesh, described as fresh beef or mutton, fell across an area roughly 100 yards long and 50 yards wide, leaving the local population both bewildered and disturbed. Many of the witnesses to this peculiar precipitation described the meat as being roughly one to three inches square, with some pieces appearing fresh while others seemed partially decomposed. Listen, I've seen some weird things in my travels, giant fiberglass animals, museums dedicated to spam, even a house made entirely of paper, but nothing quite compares to the day meat literally fell from the Kentucky sky.

Now, you might be thinking this is just another tall tale, like those stories about raining frogs or falling fish. But here's the kicker, this one's got some serious scientific documentation behind it. The Crouch family farm became ground zero for what might be history's most bizarre picnic, drawing everyone from local hunters to distinguished scientists who were eager to get their hands (and surprisingly, their taste buds) on these sky-sent samples.

Here's where it gets really interesting, and I mean the kind of interesting that makes you question everything you know about scientific methodology. Dr. L.D. Kastenbine, a Louisville chemist, actually tasted the mystery meat as part of his investigation. I know what you're thinking, who in their right mind samples unidentified meat that fell from the sky? But in the 1870s, this was apparently a totally normal way to conduct science. After his culinary adventure, he declared it was probably lung tissue from either a horse or, get this, a human infant. Talk about your unappetizing conclusions!

But wait, there's more! Nature magazine eventually stepped in with what's probably the most plausible explanation, though it's no less bizarre. Picture this: a flock of vultures, peacefully enjoying their lunch somewhere high above Kentucky, when something startles them. Now, vultures have this charming habit of lightening their load when they need to make a quick getaway, by regurgitating their last meal. So basically, the good people of Bath County got caught in what might be history's largest case of synchronized vulture vomit.

You've got to appreciate the irony here, in trying to solve one mystery, the scientists of 1876 created another. I mean, what's more fascinating: the fact that meat fell from the sky, or that the go-to method for investigating such an occurrence was to pop some in your mouth and see what happens? It's moments like these that remind me why I love digging through history's oddities, just when you think you've heard it all, you discover something that makes you realize truth really is stranger than fiction.

The story might sound too bizarre to be true, but the evidence is as solid as a well-done steak. Or in this case, as solid as partially digested vulture leftovers can be. It's one of those delightfully weird moments in history that proves science doesn't always have to be sterile and boring, sometimes it can be downright entertaining, even if it does make you lose your appetite.

The Eyewitness Accounts and Initial Public Reaction

You know how sometimes the most reliable witnesses are the ones who weren't trying to witness anything at all? That's exactly what we've got with Mrs. Allen Crouch, who was just minding her own business making soap on her porch when the sky decided to rain meat[25][24]. I've spent countless hours road-tripping across America, but I've never encountered anyone quite like Mrs. Crouch, who managed to keep her cool while describing how pieces of flesh descended "like large snowflakes" from a perfectly clear sky[25].

Here's where it gets even more fascinating, these meat chunks weren't just dropping in one spot. They were spreading out across her property like some sort of macabre confetti, sticking to fences and briers[24] and covering an area roughly 100 yards long by 50 yards wide. Now, I've seen some strange things stuck to fences in my travels, but meat from the sky? That's a new one.

Word travels fast in small towns, and Bath County, Kentucky was no exception. Before you could say "flying frankfurters," curious onlookers were flocking to the Crouch farm like it was the world's weirdest tourist attraction. By the next morning, their property had transformed into an impromptu scientific conference meets county fair, with locals all eager to get a glimpse of the mysterious sky meat.

Now, here's where the story takes a turn that makes me question the survival instincts of our ancestors. Some folks, and I'm still trying to wrap my head around this decision, actually decided to taste the mystery meat. Yes, you heard that right. In a move that would make any modern food safety inspector faint, two unnamed men sampled the flesh and declared it tasted like venison or mutton[25]. I've tried some questionable gas station snacks in my time, but even I draw the line at eating unidentified meat that fell from the sky.

The story spread like wildfire, catching the attention of newspapers across the country. The New York Times and Scientific American jumped on the meat wagon, though they couldn't quite agree on what kind of meat it was. The reports ranged from beef to lamb, deer, bear, and even horse[26]. Reading these varying accounts, I can't help but think of those modern-day social media arguments where everyone's convinced they know exactly what that viral photo shows.

Here's the really intriguing part, the local community's initial reaction wasn't just about scientific curiosity. This was 1876, after all, and plenty of folks interpreted the meat shower as some kind of divine message or supernatural event. And honestly, if chunks of meat started falling from a clear sky today, I'm pretty sure we'd have our share of creative interpretations too.

As the meat began its inevitable journey toward spoilage the following day[25], you might think people's interest would wane. But nope, if anything, it intensified the urgency to understand what had happened. Locals scrambled to collect samples for scientific examination, though I imagine handling decomposing mystery meat in the March heat wasn't exactly anyone's idea of a good time. Talk about dedication to the scientific method!

Scientific Investigations and Competing Theories

You know what's fascinating about the Kentucky Meat Shower? It's one of those rare historical events where scientists actually got their hands dirty, or in this case, meaty, right away. As someone who's spent countless hours exploring roadside oddities, I can tell you that having multiple credentialed experts investigate a weird occurrence while it's still fresh (pun intended) is pretty unusual for the 1870s[27].

Let me tell you about Dr. L. D. Kastenbine from the Louisville College of Pharmacy. This guy, and I say this with both admiration and bewilderment, decided that the best way to investigate mysterious sky meat was to pop some in his mouth[29]. Now, I've done some questionable things in the name of research during my travels, but tasting unidentified meat that fell from the sky? That's a level of scientific dedication I'm not sure I'm ready for.

But here's where it gets real interesting, once they put the meat under a microscope, they found something genuinely puzzling. The tissue structure suggested it came from either a horse's lung or, in what must have been an uncomfortable moment in the lab, possibly human infant lung tissue[29][27]. Now, before you get too creeped out, remember that 1870s microscope technology wasn't exactly state-of-the-art.

Then along comes Leopold Brandeis with what I like to call the 'space algae theory.' He took one look at the preserved samples and declared it wasn't meat at all, but Nostoc, a type of cyanobacteria that swells up after rain[29][28]. It's a creative theory, I'll give him that. But when you've got multiple people who actually tasted the stuff saying it was definitely meat, well, let's just say I'm not buying the algae angle.

But my favorite explanation? It comes from this old Ohio farmer who basically said, 'Oh yeah, that's just vulture vomit'[29][27]. Now, I know what you're thinking, that sounds like something you'd make up to mess with city folks. But here's the thing: vultures actually do this. When they need to make a quick getaway, they'll lighten their load by regurgitating their last meal. And given that vultures typically fly in flocks and could all be startled at once, say, by a loud noise, it's actually the most logical explanation we've got.

The Newark Scientific Association decided to weigh in too, confirming it was definitely animal tissue[27]. This helped shut down some of the wilder theories floating around, like supernatural phenomena or elaborate hoaxes. Though I have to say, the truth, that it was probably mass vulture vomit, is almost stranger than the supernatural explanations.

You know what I love about this whole investigation? It shows how scientific methodology has evolved. Back then, scientists were literally taste-testing mystery meat and making somewhat questionable logical leaps. Today, we'd have DNA analysis, mass spectrometry, and probably a dozen other tests I can't pronounce. But sometimes, the old-school explanation, like our farmer friend's vulture theory, turns out to be the most sensible one.

And that's what makes historical oddities like this so fascinating. We're looking at an event that sits right at the intersection of folklore and scientific investigation, where careful analysis meets "hold my beer while I taste this sky meat." It's moments like these that remind us how science and common sense sometimes take very different paths to arrive at the same conclusion.

Legacy and Impact on Modern Weather Phenomenon Studies

You'd think after nearly 150 years, we'd be done talking about the time meat fell from the Kentucky sky. But here's the thing, this bizarre incident keeps popping up in scientific discussions like that one friend who always has a weirder story to top yours. And truthfully? It's actually taught us quite a bit about how we investigate the truly strange stuff that happens in our atmosphere.

Let me tell you something I've learned from years of chasing down odd historical events, it's not just about what happened, but how people tried to figure out what happened. Those 19th-century scientists who tackled the meat shower mystery? They actually set up some pretty solid methods for investigating atmospheric anomalies. They collected samples (though maybe tasting them wasn't the best call), documented everything meticulously, and considered multiple theories before reaching conclusions[26][27].

Now, whenever something unusual falls from the sky, and trust me, it happens more often than you'd think, meteorologists still follow a similar playbook. Sure, we've added fancy equipment and sophisticated testing methods, but the basic approach those Kentucky investigators used still holds up. Collect, document, analyze, theorize, rinse and repeat[31].

But here's what really gets me excited: the meat shower has become this perfect case study for teaching critical thinking in meteorology. When I visit schools to talk about weather phenomena, I love watching students' faces when I bring up the Kentucky meat shower. First comes the "you've got to be kidding" looks, then the curiosity, and finally the realization that sometimes the most logical explanation (yes, I'm looking at you, vulture theory) can also be the weirdest[26][27].

The incident has also taught us something crucial about investigating atmospheric mysteries: sometimes you need to look beyond the atmosphere. Modern meteorologists know that what falls from the sky isn't always about weather patterns, it could be about biology (like our vulture friends), human activity, or phenomena we haven't even figured out yet[31].

You know what's really fascinating? Bath County has taken this bizarre piece of their history and turned it into something meaningful. They've got educational programs that use the meat shower to teach kids about scientific method, critical thinking, and the importance of keeping an open mind when investigating the unexplained. I've visited their local museum, and let me tell you, they've done an amazing job of turning a pretty gross historical event into an engaging lesson about science[30].

In the modern era of weather science, the Kentucky meat shower stands as this wonderful reminder that sometimes the most valuable scientific lessons come from the weirdest places. It's pushed meteorologists to maintain what I call a "respectfully skeptical" approach, taking unusual phenomena seriously while methodically working through possible explanations[26][27].

Every time I tell this story at scientific conferences (and yes, it still comes up at meteorological meetings), someone inevitably points out how it perfectly demonstrates the evolution of scientific investigation. We've gone from tasting mystery meat to using advanced spectrometry and DNA analysis, but the fundamental approach, observe, document, analyze, explain, remains the same[31]. And sometimes, just sometimes, the explanation still turns out to be as bizarre as vulture vomit falling from the sky. You know what keeps me up at night? Not the thought of meat falling from the sky, though that's pretty unsettling, but the realization that sometimes our most rational explanations are just as bizarre as the mysteries they solve. I mean, who would've thought "synchronized vulture vomit" would end up being the most logical answer to one of Kentucky's strangest moments?

What I love about the Kentucky Meat Shower isn't just its sheer weirdness, though that's certainly part of its charm. It's how this incident perfectly captures that beautiful moment in scientific history when we were transitioning from "let's taste it and see what happens" to actual methodical investigation. Those early scientists, despite their questionable sampling methods, were onto something important. They showed us that even the most outlandish events deserve serious scientific scrutiny.

And here's what really gets me: those 19th-century investigators didn't just shrug and label it a hoax or divine intervention. They rolled up their sleeves (hopefully before handling the mystery meat) and got to work. They collected samples, documented everything meticulously, and considered multiple theories, even the wildest ones, before settling on what's probably the truth. Sure, their methods might make modern scientists cringe, but their dedication to finding rational explanations? That's timeless.

Every time I share this story during my roadside adventures, someone inevitably asks, "But what if it was something else?" And that's exactly the kind of questioning these historical oddities should inspire. Because in the end, the Kentucky Meat Shower isn't just about mysterious flesh falling from the sky, it's about how we approach the unexplained, how we balance skepticism with open-mindedness, and how sometimes the truth is even stranger than the mystery itself.

So next time you're driving through Kentucky and spot some vultures circling overhead, maybe give them a little salute. After all, their ancestors might have been responsible for one of history's most peculiar scientific investigations. Just don't park your car directly under them, some scientific experiments don't need repeating.

Chapter 5

The Lost Roman Legion

How 10,000 Soldiers Ended Up in Ancient China

IN THE HARSH DESERTS of Central Asia, thousands of miles from the familiar streets of Rome, an entire Roman legion vanished into the mists of history. Their incredible journey would span continents, cross the boundaries of empires, and create one of history's most fascinating mysteries, the story of how thousands of Roman soldiers may have ended up serving as border guards in ancient China. Picture this, these battle-hardened Roman soldiers, who'd spent their lives patrolling the familiar streets of Rome, suddenly finding themselves marching through landscapes they'd only heard about in travelers' tales. The Parthians, after delivering that crushing defeat at Carrhae, didn't just imprison these legionaries, they put them to work as border guards on their eastern frontier. But here's where things get really interesting, folks. These Roman soldiers, already way out of their comfort zone, kept getting pushed further and further east until they ended up doing something absolutely mind-bending, they crossed paths with one of the most powerful empires in history: Han Dynasty China.

Now, I've spent countless hours poring over Han Dynasty records (trust me, they were meticulous record-keepers), and they describe something that'll make your head spin. Their chronicles mention these peculiar foreign troops who fought using tactics that were decidedly un-Asian, we're talking classic Roman testudo formations and European-style fortification techniques. It's like finding a pizza place in ancient China, it just shouldn't be there, but somehow it is!

But wait, it gets better. The archaeological evidence is like a treasure trail of breadcrumbs leading right to this wild conclusion. We're talking Roman-style bronze coins popping up in Chinese tombs, pottery that looks like it came straight from a Mediterranean workshop, and buildings that would look right at home in ancient Rome. And get this, DNA studies in the region have turned up some surprisingly European genetic markers among the local population. It's as if these Roman soldiers didn't just pass through, they set up shop, settled down, and became part of the local community.

Think about that for a second. These guys went from fighting for the glory of Rome to becoming cultural ambassadors on the other side of the known world. They weren't just soldiers anymore; they were unwitting pioneers of one of history's most remarkable cultural exchanges. We're talking about people who probably started their military careers dreaming of returning to Rome as heroes, only to end up leaving their mark on the opposite end of the ancient world.

The evidence suggests these Romans didn't just maintain their military discipline; they adapted and thrived in their new environment. They combined Roman engineering with Chinese innovations, created hybrid architectural styles, and probably exchanged everything from military tactics to recipes. It's like ancient fusion cuisine, but with swords and sandals!

The more you dig into this story, the more it starts to feel less like a historical footnote and more like an ancient version of the greatest road trip ever, except instead of a beaten-up van, these guys had their Roman shields and sandals, and their GPS was probably a series of very confused local guides pointing east. It's a reminder that history isn't just about battles and emperors, it's about people who, whether by choice or circumstance, end up on incredible journeys that reshape our understanding of the ancient world.

The Battle of Carrhae: Rome's Eastern Disaster

You know what's wild about ancient Rome? Sometimes their biggest disasters came from good old-fashioned overconfidence. Take Marcus Licinius Crassus, for instance. Here's a guy who was basically the Jeff Bezos of ancient Rome[32], but apparently being the richest dude in town wasn't enough for him. He wanted some of that sweet military glory his buddies Julius Caesar and Pompey were hogging[35].

So picture this, it's 53 BCE, and Crassus decides to march seven Roman legions (that's about 40,000 guys) into Parthian territory like he's taking a stroll through the Forum. I mean, how hard could it be to beat some eastern horse riders, right? Spoiler alert: pretty darn hard, as it turns out.

The Parthians had this general named Surena who was basically playing 4D chess while Crassus was still figuring out checkers. Instead of meeting the Romans head-on like they expected, Surena brought out his secret weapons, mounted archers who could shoot arrows while riding backwards (yeah, that was a thing) and these heavily armored cavalry units called cataphracts that were basically ancient tanks[35].

The battle went down near Carrhae (that's modern-day Harran in Turkey), and let me tell you, it was less of a battle and more of a masterclass in "How Not to Fight Parthians 101." While the Romans were lugging around their heavy infantry equipment in the scorching desert, Surena's mounted archers just kept circling them like kids playing keep-away, peppering them with arrows from a distance that the Romans couldn't reach[35].

Here's where it gets really messy. Crassus's son Publius led this desperate cavalry charge to try to break the cycle of death by arrows. The Parthians just went "That's cute" and pulled their signature move, pretending to retreat, then turning around and absolutely demolishing their pursuers. And because ancient warfare apparently wasn't brutal enough, they put poor Publius's head on a spear and paraded it in front of his dad's troops[35]. Talk about psychological warfare.

By the end of this disaster, 20,000 Romans were dead, another 10,000 got captured, and the rest probably wished they'd called in sick that day[32][34]. As for Crassus himself? Well, he got himself killed during some sketchy peace talks, and the Parthians allegedly poured molten gold down his throat, a pretty on-the-nose way of saying "How's that greed working out for you?"[34]

But here's where it gets really interesting. Those 10,000 captured Romans? They didn't just disappear into some ancient POW camp. The Parthians sent them east, way east, to guard their frontier. Some historians think these guys might have ended up as far as China, which if true, means this military disaster accidentally kicked off one of history's most epic road trips.

And the ripple effects? Oh boy. Crassus's death threw Rome's political scene into chaos, basically setting up the Caesar vs. Pompey showdown that would turn the Republic into an Empire[33]. Plus, losing all those soldiers left Rome's eastern borders about as secure as a screen door on a submarine, leading to years of Parthian raids[33].

It just goes to show you, sometimes the worst military disasters come not from facing a superior force, but from underestimating your enemy and overestimating your own abilities. That, and maybe don't invade Parthia without a solid plan for dealing with horse archers. Just ask Mark Antony how that worked out for him later, but that's a story for another day.

The Long March East: From Parthia to Han Dynasty China

Hey there, history fans! Ever wondered what happens when you take thousands of battle-hardened Roman soldiers and drop them into the ancient equivalent of a cross-continental road trip? Well, buckle up, because I'm about to tell you about one of history's most incredible forced migrations.

After the Parthians finished celebrating their victory at Carrhae, they had to figure out what to do with roughly 10,000 captured Roman soldiers[38]. Now, most armies would've just executed their prisoners, but the Parthians were thinking outside the box. They looked at these highly trained veterans and thought, "Hey, why waste all that military expertise?" So they came up with a plan that was either brilliant or completely bonkers, they decided to march these Romans to their eastern frontier.

Let me paint you a picture of this journey. We're talking about crossing some of the most extreme terrain in the ancient world. These guys, used to the comfortable Mediterranean climate, had to trek across scorching deserts, scale snow-capped mountain passes, and navigate valleys that would make a mountain goat nervous. And they weren't exactly doing this with Google Maps and rest stops along the way.

Initially, these Roman POWs found themselves manning Parthian frontier posts[38], dealing with raids from Central Asian nomads. But here's where the story gets really wild. The Han Chinese started noticing some very un-Asian military tactics showing up in their battles. During the Battle of Zhizhi in 36 BCE, Chinese general Chen Tang ran into soldiers using this weird "fish-scale" formation[36,37,38,39]. Any Roman would've recognized this instantly, it was the famous testudo (tortoise) formation, a Roman military signature move!

The Han Dynasty folks were pretty impressed by these mysterious western warriors. So impressed, in fact, that they apparently settled some of them in a town called Liqian (in modern-day Gansu province). Here's a fun linguistic twist, Liqian was actually one of the Chinese terms for Alexandria and, by extension, Rome itself[39]. Talk about a coincidence!

Now, I know what you're thinking, surely there must be some genetic evidence of Romans in modern China, right? Well, that's where things get tricky. Modern DNA studies haven't found any smoking gun proof of Roman ancestry in the region[37]. But before you dismiss the whole story, remember that we're talking about a relatively small group of men who lived there over 2,000 years ago. Finding their genetic footprint would be like trying to find a specific grain of sand on a beach.

What makes this story so fascinating isn't just the epic journey, it's what it tells us about ancient globalization. Think about it: Roman military techniques showing up in Chinese battles, cultural exchange happening across thousands of miles, and soldiers from the Mediterranean adapting to life in East Asia. This wasn't just a simple prisoner transfer; it was an accidental cultural exchange program that spanned the length of Asia!

The story of these displaced legionaries is like something out of a historical road trip movie, except nobody signed up for this particular adventure. They started as proud Roman soldiers, became Parthian border guards, and potentially ended up as respected warriors in Han China. Talk about a career change! It just goes to show that sometimes life's most incredible journeys aren't the ones we choose, but the ones that choose us.

Archaeological Evidence: The Roman Presence in Ancient China

Let me tell you about my favorite part of this whole lost legion mystery, the stuff we can actually dig up and hold in our hands. You see, back in the 1990s, some archaeologists got pretty excited when they found these fortifications in a place called Liqian (modern-day Zhelaizhai) that looked about as Chinese as pasta carbonara[39]. We're talking defensive structures that would've made any Roman military engineer feel right at home, complete with those signature wooden stakes arranged in patterns that practically screamed "I learned this in Rome!"[36]

Now, here's where it gets really interesting. Someone dug up this helmet with Chinese characters that basically said "I surrendered", which, let's be honest, is probably not something you'd want engraved on your battle gear unless you had a really interesting story to tell. And right nearby? A Roman-style water pot that looked like it took a wrong turn somewhere around the Euphrates[36].

But wait, there's more! The locals in Zhelaizhai have been pointing at their mirrors for generations, noting some decidedly un-Chinese features, we're talking brown hair, blue or green eyes, the kind of looks that would've turned heads in ancient China[40][36]. When scientists first started poking around with DNA tests in the early 2000s, they got pretty excited about finding some Caucasian genetic markers[40]. Though, full disclosure, later studies suggested these European traits probably had more to do with the Silk Road being history's longest-running multicultural mixer than direct Roman ancestry[41].

Here's the thing about archaeology, though, sometimes what we don't find is just as interesting as what we do. For all our digging, we haven't found any Roman coins stamped with emperors' faces, no distinctly Roman weapons, and no Latin inscriptions saying "Marcus was here"[36]. It's like trying to prove your friend visited when they forgot to sign the guestbook but left their favorite coffee mug behind.

The most fascinating bit? The locals have totally embraced this maybe-Roman heritage. Liqian's turned into this quirky tourist spot where you can see Roman-style statues next to traditional Chinese architecture[36]. It's like a historical fusion restaurant where no one's quite sure about the original recipe, but everyone's enjoying the meal anyway.

Sure, most historians and geneticists these days aren't fully convinced about a direct Roman settlement in Liqian[41][39]. But you know what? The physical evidence we do have tells us something even more interesting, that the ancient world was way more interconnected than our history books sometimes let on. These artifacts, whether they belonged to lost Roman legionaries or Silk Road traders, show us that people were mixing, mingling, and swapping stories (and probably recipes) across thousands of miles long before anyone dreamed up social media.

It's kind of like being a historical detective, we might not have enough evidence to close the case completely, but the clues we do have paint a picture of a world where cultures weren't just bumping into each other, they were doing the ancient equivalent of a group chat across continents. And isn't that way cooler than just finding a bunch of Roman soldiers' sandals in the Chinese desert? You know what gets me every time I think about those lost Roman legionaries? It wasn't just some military mishap, it was the start of one of history's most epic unplanned adventures. We're talking about guys who probably started their morning thinking "Just another day guarding the Empire" and ended up being accidental pioneers of East-West relations.

Look, I'll level with you, we may never know exactly how many Romans made it all the way to China. The evidence is like trying to piece together a 2,000-year-old jigsaw puzzle where most of the pieces got scattered across the largest continent on Earth. But what we do know is pretty mind-blowing: Roman military formations showing up in Chinese battles, mystery soldiers with Mediterranean features guarding Han Dynasty borders, and archaeological findings that make archaeologists scratch their heads and say "Huh, that's not supposed to be here."

Here's what I find truly fascinating, these soldiers didn't just survive; they adapted. They took their Roman know-how and mixed it with local techniques, creating this amazing cultural fusion that nobody planned for. It's like they accidentally invented ancient world fusion cuisine, but with military tactics and architecture instead of food.

Their journey challenges everything we think we know about how isolated ancient civilizations were from each other. It turns out the ancient world was more like a really slow-moving Internet, where ideas, techniques, and yes, even lost legions could end up halfway across the known world. These guys were like the ancient world's first unintentional influencers, spreading Roman military innovation one forced march at a time.

So next time someone tells you globalization is a modern thing, just remember those Roman soldiers who went from defending the streets of Rome to possibly training troops in ancient China. Now that's what I call a career change! Their story reminds us that sometimes history's most amazing tales aren't about the battles won or lost, but about the incredible journeys people make when life throws them the ultimate curveball.

Chapter 6

The Phantom Time Hypothesis

Did the Middle Ages Really Happen?

T IME ITSELF SEEMS STRAIGHTFORWARD enough, sixty seconds in a minute, twenty-four hours in a day, and history marching steadily forward from past to present. But what if someone told you that nearly three hundred years of history were completely fabricated, and that Charlemagne was as fictional as a character in a fairy tale? I'll admit that as someone who spends way too much time hunting down roadside oddities and questioning accepted truths, I find this whole Phantom Time business absolutely fascinating. German historian Heribert Illig really went all in with this theory back in '91, claiming a massive medieval cover-up erased nearly 300 years from existence. Talk about your ultimate historical heist!

Now, I've seen some wild theories in my travels across America's backroads, but this one takes the medieval cake. The basic idea goes something like this: sometime around the 16th century, when folks were switching from the Julian to Gregorian calendar, Emperor Otto III and Pope Sylvester II supposedly cooked up this elaborate scheme to fake three centuries worth of history. According to Illig, they whipped up fake documents, invented historical figures (including good ol' Charlemagne), and somehow got everyone from monks to merchants to play along. It's like a conspiracy theory meets historical fan fiction!

Here's where it gets really interesting though, and trust me, I've spent countless late nights piecing this puzzle together. Modern scientists and historians have had an absolute field day debunking this one. See, those medieval folks might not have had smartphones, but they were pretty good at tracking celestial events. We've got astronomical records from multiple civilizations, Chinese, Islamic, European, all matching up perfectly during those supposedly 'phantom' years. It's like having timestamped photos from different people at the same party, pretty hard to fake!

But my favorite part? The archaeological evidence. It's like finding breadcrumbs through time, except instead of bread, we're talking about coins, buildings, and artifacts that line up perfectly with that 'missing' period. Carbon dating doesn't lie, folks, unless you want to argue that half-life itself was in on the conspiracy! And don't even get me started on the cross-cultural documentation. We're talking about records from civilizations that barely knew each other existed, all independently confirming events during these supposedly 'phantom' years.

What makes this whole theory so captivating isn't just its audacity, it's how it pushes us to question how we know what we know about history. As someone who's spent countless hours tracking down America's weirdest historical markers, I can tell you that proving the past happened is a lot trickier than you'd think. But that's also what makes it so exciting! Every piece of evidence is like a clue in this massive historical scavenger hunt, leading us closer to the truth.

The Phantom Time Hypothesis turns out to be less about missing centuries and more about how we piece together our understanding of the past. It's kind of like trying to solve a gigantic jigsaw puzzle where all the pieces are scattered across different continents and centuries. And let me tell you, after chasing down enough historical mysteries on America's backroads, I've learned that the real satisfaction isn't in finding conspiracy theories, it's in discovering how all these different pieces of evidence fit together to tell us stories about who we were and how we got here.

The Origins and Claims of the Phantom Time Hypothesis

Boy, do I love a good historical mystery, but this one's a real doozy! Picture this: it's 1991, and German historian Heribert Illig drops a bombshell that would make even the most seasoned conspiracy theorists do a double-take[43] [44] [45] [46]. He claims that nearly 300 years of medieval history, from 614 to 911 CE, never actually happened. That's right, according to Illig, we all collectively imagined three centuries worth of history!

Now, as someone who's spent countless hours tracking down America's weirdest historical markers and roadside attractions, I thought I'd seen it all. But Illig's theory? It's like suggesting someone hit the cosmic delete key on the Middle Ages! The mastermind behind this alleged grand deception? None other than Holy Roman Emperor Otto III, who supposedly teamed up with Pope Sylvester II and Byzantine Emperor Constantine VII for history's greatest cover-up[44] [46] [47]. Their motivation? Apparently, these powerful figures wanted to position themselves at the prestigious year 1000 CE instead of the less impressive 996 CE. Talk about an extreme case of calendar FOMO!

Illig's "evidence" is where things get really interesting. He points to what he sees as suspiciously consistent architecture during the "phantom" period[45] [46], kind of like accusing medieval builders of lacking creativity! He also gets really worked up about some supposed quirks in the transition between the Julian and Gregorian calendars[44] [46]. But his piece de resistance? Claiming that Charlemagne, one of history's most famous rulers, was completely made up[44][45][46]. That's right, according to Illig, medieval Europe's most celebrated emperor was basically historical fanfiction!

Here's the thing though, and I've seen enough weird history to know when something doesn't add up, this theory falls apart faster than a cardboard castle in a rainstorm. When actual historians and scientists got their hands on it, they found more holes than in my favorite pair of road trip jeans[44]. We've got independent historical records from cultures all over Europe, Asia, and the Americas that line up perfectly with our traditional timeline. It's like having thousands of witnesses all telling the same story, pretty hard to fake that kind of coordination across continents!

What really fascinates me about the Phantom Time Hypothesis isn't the theory itself (which, let's be honest, is about as solid as a chocolate teapot), but what it teaches us about how we verify history. Think about it, we can prove these centuries existed through astronomy, archaeology, linguistics, and documents from completely different civilizations. It's like having a historical jigsaw puzzle where all the pieces fit perfectly, no matter which angle you look at them from.

In my travels across America's backroads, I've learned that the best stories aren't always the wildest ones, they're the ones that help us understand how we know what we know. The Phantom Time Hypothesis might be wrong, but it accidentally showed us something pretty amazing: our understanding of history is built on evidence that's more interconnected and reliable than we often realize. And personally, I find that way more exciting than any conspiracy theory could ever be!

Archaeological and Documentary Evidence from the "Missing" Period

I've seen some pretty wild things in my roadside wanderings, but nothing quite matches the mountain of evidence that crushes this "missing time" theory like a monster truck at a demolition derby. Let me walk you through what actual historians and scientists have uncovered, it's way more fascinating than any conspiracy theory!

First up, let's talk trees. You know how trees add a ring for each year they grow? Well, these woody time-keepers have been quietly documenting history for centuries[49]. Scientists have pieced together continuous tree ring records that run right through our supposedly "phantom" years without so much as a hiccup. Unless medieval conspirators figured out how to fake tree rings (spoiler alert: they didn't), we've got some pretty solid proof these years were as real as the coffee I'm drinking right now.

But wait, there's more! Remember those medieval stargazers who kept detailed records of eclipses and comets? Modern astronomers have done the math, and guess what? Those celestial events happened exactly when and where our ancestors said they did. It's like having a cosmic timestamp on history! When Pliny the Elder wrote about watching a solar eclipse in 59 AD, he wasn't just spinning yarns, modern calculations prove that an eclipse happened right on schedule.

Now, let's dig into something really cool, actual stuff from these supposedly non-existent years. I'm talking coins, pottery, buildings, and tools that archaeologists have unearthed in perfectly dated layers of dirt. Each artifact tells a story of gradual development, like how Carolingian art didn't just pop up overnight like some historical jack-in-the-box. These things evolved over time, leaving a clear trail through those allegedly "missing" centuries[49].

Here's what really seals the deal for me, all these different civilizations keeping their own records at the same time. While Europe was supposedly living through these "fake" years, the Tang Dynasty in China and scholars of the Islamic Golden Age were busy documenting everything from astronomical events to trade agreements[48]. The chances of multiple civilizations coordinating such an elaborate hoax across vast distances and language barriers? About as likely as finding a dinosaur at a drive-through!

The Anglo-Saxon Chronicle is particularly fascinating, it's like a medieval newspaper that lines up perfectly with records from across Europe and beyond[49]. Meanwhile, brilliant minds like Al-Khwarizmi were making groundbreaking mathematical discoveries and tracking celestial events that would later find their way to European scholars. These weren't imaginary scientists working in phantom time, they were real people making real contributions to human knowledge.

You know what's really wild? The more you dig into the evidence, the more you realize just how interconnected human history really is. It's like following the threads of the world's biggest tapestry, pull on one string in medieval Europe, and you'll find it connected to China, the Middle East, and beyond. As someone who's spent years chasing down historical oddities, I can tell you that sometimes the real story is way more interesting than any conspiracy theory could ever be.

Scientific Refutation: Astronomical Records and Carbon Dating

Let me tell you something wild, if you're going to try to fake three centuries of history, you'd better make sure the stars are in on your conspiracy! As someone who's spent countless nights getting lost under dark prairie skies while chasing down America's oddest historical markers, I've gained a deep appreciation for how the cosmos keeps its own perfectly accurate calendar.

See, those medieval astronomers weren't just casual stargazers, they were scientific record-keepers extraordinaire[50]. When they documented solar eclipses, comets, and other celestial events, they were unknowingly creating an astronomical paper trail that modern scientists can verify with mind-boggling precision. Take the Chinese astronomers who meticulously recorded a supernova in 1054 CE (smack in the middle of our supposedly phantom time), their description matches perfectly with what we now know as the Crab Nebula[50].

But here's what really blows my mind, because astronomy follows strict mathematical rules, we can calculate exactly when and where these events happened. It's like having a cosmic time machine! When medieval Islamic scholars wrote about observing specific planetary alignments, modern astronomers can fire up their computers and confirm, "Yep, Jupiter was exactly where they said it was on that date!"

And don't even get me started on radiocarbon dating! As someone who's held genuine historical artifacts (under strict supervision, of course), I can tell you there's something magical about being able to scientifically determine an object's age. Carbon-14 doesn't care about conspiracy theories, it just keeps doing its decay thing at a perfectly predictable rate[50]. When scientists test artifacts from these supposedly phantom years, guess what? The dates line up exactly where they should.

Here's the real kicker, all these different lines of evidence work together like the world's most elaborate historical jigsaw puzzle. Tree rings match radiocarbon dates, which align with astronomical observations, which sync up with archaeological findings, which correspond to written records from multiple civilizations[43][50]. It's like catching the same amazing sunset from different spots across the country, each perspective confirms the others.

I've seen some impressive coordination in my travels, like that time I watched a perfectly choreographed classic car parade through small-town Kansas, but getting multiple civilizations, celestial bodies, and atomic decay to all fake the same three centuries? That would be a feat even more impossible than finding decent coffee at 3 AM in the middle of nowhere!

The simple truth is, these medieval years were as real as the road beneath my wheels. The stars themselves tell us so, and they've been keeping time a lot longer than any of us. Sometimes the most extraordinary thing about history isn't the conspiracies we imagine, but how remarkably well we can verify what actually happened. Now that's what I call a stellar conclusion! You know what I love most about chasing down historical mysteries? It's not just about debunking wild theories, it's about discovering how incredibly interconnected our past really is. This Phantom Time business got me thinking about all the different ways we can verify history, and let me tell you, it's way more fascinating than any conspiracy theory.

Throughout my adventures tracking down America's weirdest historical sites, I've discovered that the real magic happens when you start connecting the dots. Sure, it's fun to imagine some elaborate medieval conspiracy, but the truth is even more amazing. Think about it, we've got tree rings in Europe matching up with Chinese astronomical records, Islamic mathematical treatises syncing perfectly with European documents, and radiocarbon dating confirming it all. It's like the world's most elaborate historical scavenger hunt, with clues scattered across continents and centuries!

What really gets me excited is how this whole investigation shows just how sophisticated our ancestors were. These weren't just people fumbling around in the dark ages, they were brilliant observers who kept meticulous records of everything from solar eclipses to trade agreements. And the best part? Their observations stood the test of time. Modern scientists can fire up their computers and confirm that yes, that comet appeared exactly when and where the medieval astronomers said it would.

But here's my favorite takeaway from this whole phantom time adventure: history isn't just a bunch of dusty facts in textbooks. It's a living puzzle where every piece, from tree rings to astronomical charts, from ancient coins to crumbling manuscripts, fits together to tell us an incredible story about who we are and where we came from. And isn't that way cooler than any conspiracy theory could ever be?

So next time someone tries to tell you that three centuries of history were made up, just remember, the stars themselves disagree, and they've been keeping time a lot longer than any of us. Now if you'll excuse me, I've got another historical oddity to chase down somewhere off Route 66!

Chapter 7

The Tunguska Event
The Day Siberia Exploded

O N THE MORNING OF June 30, 1908, the skies above Siberia erupted in a blinding flash that would puzzle scientists for generations to come. The explosion, equivalent to roughly 1,000 times the power of the atomic bomb dropped on Hiroshima, flattened an area of forest roughly the size of modern-day London, yet left no impact crater. The puzzling event would become known as the Tunguska Event, named after the nearby Stony Tunguska River, and would spark over a century of scientific investigation and speculation that, quite frankly, still keeps me up at night sometimes. Think about it, we're talking about something that packed enough punch to knock trees flat across an area bigger than my entire road trip through Texas last summer (and let me tell you, that was one long drive).

I've got to tell you, every time I dive into the eyewitness accounts from those Evenki tribes and Russian settlers, I get goosebumps. Imagine stepping out for your morning coffee only to see what they described as this otherworldly blue fireball, brighter than the sun itself, streaking across the sky. Then BOOM, your windows shake, the ground trembles, and suddenly you're living in a real-life science fiction movie.

Now, here's where it gets really weird, folks. The explosion was so massive it leveled an estimated 80 million trees in a pattern that looked like a giant had played pick-up sticks from above. Picture this: trees near ground zero were standing there like nature's own telephone poles, completely stripped of their branches and bark. The strangest part? Despite all this destruction, nobody could find a crater. It's like whatever caused this cosmic temper tantrum simply vanished into thin air.

When Leonid Kulik finally made it out there in 1927 (talk about delayed response, but hey, have you ever tried navigating remote Siberia during a civil war?), most of the evidence had already started growing over. But even with nature trying to cover its tracks, the devastation was clear as day. You could still see exactly where this mysterious force had redecorated the Siberian landscape.

You know what really gets me? The whole thing was so powerful that seismic stations across Eurasia picked it up, and the pressure waves circled the Earth. Twice. Let that sink in for a minute. We're talking about an explosion that literally made the planet ring like a bell. The skies lit up so bright that folks in London, that's 3,500 miles away, could read their newspapers at midnight. If that doesn't make you question what else might be floating around in space, I don't know what will.

I've spent countless nights poring over scientific papers, theories, and historical accounts, trying to wrap my head around what actually happened that summer morning in 1908. Was it a meteor? A chunk of antimatter? A small comet? A visitor from another world? (Hey, I'm not saying it was aliens, but...) The truth is, we still don't have all the answers. And maybe that's what makes this story so fascinating, it reminds us that sometimes the universe can put on a show that leaves even our brightest minds scratching their heads.

This cosmic mystery has shaped how we think about planetary defense and our vulnerability to space rocks. These days, we've got teams of scientists tracking potentially hazardous asteroids, running simulations, and making plans for when (not if) we spot another big one heading our way. Because if Tunguska taught us anything, it's that sometimes the biggest threats come from above, and they don't always leave a forwarding address.

The Eyewitness Accounts and Initial Reports

Let me tell you about S. Semenov, who was just trying to enjoy his breakfast at the Vanavara Trading Post when the universe decided to throw him the wildest curveball imaginable. Picture this: you're sitting there, probably wondering if you should have another cup of tea, when suddenly the sky literally splits in two. Not metaphorically, we're talking about an actual wall of fire spreading across the northern horizon like someone had taken a cosmic blowtorch to the heavens.[51]

Semenov, who'd soon become our star witness in this cosmic drama, said it got so hot he felt like his shirt was on fire. And just when he thought things couldn't get any weirder, the sky did something I can only describe as hitting the universal pause button, it "shut closed." Then BOOM! The poor guy got thrown several meters through the air like a rag doll. I've had some rough mornings in my time, but this definitely takes the cake.[51]

Now, the folks at the Evenki settlements closer to ground zero? They had it even worse. Imagine losing entire herds of reindeer, we're talking about a thousand animals, scattered across the landscape like nature's morbid connect-the-dots. The Evenki hunters' accounts are particularly valuable here because they knew this land like the back of their hands. One hunter, Okhchen, later became the MVP for scientific expeditions, guiding researchers through the devastation.[53]

Here's where it gets really wild, this thing wasn't just a local spectacle. In Kirensk, a guy named Ivan Suvorov described what started as an increasingly loud noise traveling across the sky, culminating in this massive fiery column around 7:15 AM.[52] Meanwhile, about

200 kilometers away at the Kezhma settlement, some farmer watched fire pouring from the sky that was "brighter than the sun" (because regular sunlight apparently wasn't bright enough), followed by explosions that sounded like artillery practice.[54]

One of my favorite accounts comes from this train engineer who was nowhere near the blast site. The guy felt such strong vibrations that he stopped his locomotive, convinced it had jumped the tracks. Can you imagine explaining that one to your supervisor? "Sorry I'm late, boss, but I thought the universe was trying to derail us." He even demanded an inspection at the next station, though they didn't find anything wrong.[53]

At the Vadecara Trading Station, poor Kosolapov had his own bizarre encounter when his stove door decided to go rogue, it flew clean off its hinges and landed on a bed! The heat was so intense he thought his roof was on fire and found himself clutching his ears in panic.[53]

What makes these accounts particularly fascinating isn't just their dramatic content, it's how consistently they line up. Whether you were a hunter, a trader, or just someone trying to get through their morning routine, everyone described the same key elements: that blinding light, the overwhelming heat, those earth-shaking shock waves. It's like they all witnessed the same cosmic horror show from different seats in the house.[51 52 53 54]

When Leonid Kulik finally showed up in 1927 for the first major scientific expedition, these eyewitness accounts proved invaluable. Think about it, trying to find the epicenter of an explosion 19 years after the fact, in a forest that was already starting to heal itself? That's like trying to find your keys in a forest, except the forest is the size of Rhode Island. Without these detailed accounts of which way the trees fell and where the devastation was worst, they might still be searching today.[51 53]

The local newspapers at the time were absolutely stumped. I mean, how do you even begin to report something like this? Their interpretations ranged from divine intervention to natural disaster, but nobody could quite wrap their heads around what had just happened in their backyard. And honestly, can you blame them? We're still scratching our heads about it today, and we've got satellites and advanced physics on our side.[51 52 54]

Scientific Theories and Investigations

Look, I've spent more nights than I care to admit falling down internet rabbit holes about what exactly happened over Siberia that morning, and let me tell you, trying to sort through all the scientific theories is like playing cosmic detective with a deck of cards where half the evidence went missing. The leading explanation? Picture a cosmic bowling ball, we're talking about an asteroid roughly the size of a football field, screaming through Earth's atmosphere at speeds between 11-20 kilometers per second. That's fast enough to make your morning commute look like you're moving in slow motion.[57][55]

Here's where it gets fascinating: when Leonid Kulik first trudged out there in 1927 (bless his determined heart), he was absolutely certain he'd find a massive crater filled with meteorite bits. I mean, wouldn't you expect one after an explosion that powerful? Instead, he found... nothing. Well, not exactly nothing, he found millions of trees knocked flat in this bizarre butterfly pattern, like nature's version of crop circles. But no crater, no space rocks, just an enormous patch of devastation that looked like some cosmic giant had played pickup sticks.[56][53]

Now, this is where the real detective work begins. Scientists did find these tiny glass beads in the soil containing nickel and iridium, elements you typically find in meteorites.[56] It's like finding cosmic breadcrumbs, except these breadcrumbs tell us something hit us from space, but then decided to play hide and seek.

Here's my favorite theory (and trust me, I've heard some doozies): picture this massive iron asteroid, about as big as a football stadium, doing a cosmic drive-by. Instead of crashing straight into Earth, it might have skipped through our atmosphere like a stone across a pond before heading back into space.[55] Talk about a close call!

Of course, there's also the comet theory, which honestly makes a lot of sense when you think about it. Comets are basically dirty space snowballs, they'd vaporize completely in our atmosphere, leaving no crater. Plus, this whole thing went down during the Beta Taurid meteor shower, and people reported those weirdly glowing skies as far away as London for days afterward.[57]

Modern computer simulations have helped narrow things down considerably. They've shown that an icy comet would've vaporized too quickly to cause all that damage, while an iron body could've created that massive shockwave without leaving much behind.[55] The math seems to support an asteroid airburst theory, suggesting something around 120 feet across exploding several miles up.

But you know what really gets me? Those pressure waves from the blast circled the Earth twice. Twice! Barographs as far away as England picked them up. And remember those bright skies I mentioned? People in London, that's thousands of miles away, could read newspapers at midnight.[55][57] The amount of energy this thing released makes your average thunderstorm look like a firecracker.

Look, we still don't have all the answers. We're not even sure exactly what the Tunguska object was, why there's no impact crater, or if there might be some wild process we haven't figured out yet. But that's what makes science so exciting, sometimes the best discoveries come from the mysteries we haven't solved yet.

I keep thinking about those tiny glass beads in the soil, those pressure waves circling the globe, and those trees laid out in that strange butterfly pattern. It's like the universe left us a puzzle, and we're still finding new pieces to this day. Every advance in technology gives us new tools to look at this century-old mystery with fresh eyes. And maybe that's the real lesson here, sometimes the most fascinating scientific discoveries aren't the answers we find, but the questions that keep us searching.

Cultural Impact and Modern Understanding

You know what keeps me up at night about Tunguska? Not just the cosmic fireworks or the flattened forest, it's how this event fundamentally changed our relationship with the sky above. When I'm road-tripping across the country, stopping at those little diners where conversations flow as freely as the coffee, someone inevitably brings up Tunguska when we start talking about space. It's become this perfect cocktail of verifiable science and enduring mystery that captures imaginations like nothing else.

The Evenki people, who've called this region home for generations, initially saw the explosion through a completely different lens than we do today. In their oral histories, passed down through generations, they speak of Ogdy, their thunder god, showing his displeasure with humans encroaching too far into his domain. The story goes that Ogdy sent a powerful message by clearing the forest and scattering the reindeer herds, a divine reset button, if you will.[57]

But here's what fascinates me most: this event didn't just leave physical scars on the landscape, it permanently altered how we think about our cosmic vulnerability. Before Tunguska, the idea of objects from space posing a serious threat to Earth was mostly the stuff of science fiction. After Tunguska? Well, let's just say it gave everyone a cosmic wake-up call.[58]

The scientific community's delayed response, taking almost two decades before launching the first major expedition, actually worked in an interesting way. It allowed this perfect brew of folk tales, scientific theories, and wild speculation to simmer together, creating this rich cultural stew that still flavors our discussions today. Every time I visit a small-town museum or roadside attraction that mentions Tunguska, I'm amazed at how the story has evolved while keeping its core mystery intact.[59]

Case in point: Asteroid Day. Who would've thought that a random Tuesday in June would become an annual reminder of our cosmic vulnerability? The fact that we picked June 30th, the anniversary of Tunguska, tells you everything you need to know about how this single event shaped our understanding of cosmic threats.[59]

I've noticed something interesting in my travels, Tunguska has become this sort of universal measuring stick for potential cosmic disasters. Whenever scientists talk about asteroid risks or planetary defense, they inevitably mention Tunguska. It's our go-to reference point, like saying something is "as tall as the Empire State Building" or "as heavy as a blue whale."[57]

Here's the thing about Tunguska that really gets me: while science has pretty much settled on the asteroid airburst theory, explaining the basic mechanics of what happened that morning, the event still manages to captivate us. Maybe it's because it combines two things humans find irresistible, tangible evidence and lingering mystery. We can measure the devastation, analyze the soil samples, and model the explosion, but we still can't tell you exactly what that object was or show you a single piece of it.[58]

And perhaps that's why Tunguska remains such a powerful story. It reminds us that sometimes the most important scientific discoveries aren't just about finding answers, they're about understanding just how much we still have to learn about our cosmic neighborhood. Every time I look up at the night sky during my road trips, I can't help but wonder what other celestial surprises might be out there, waiting to make their own dramatic entrance.[59]You know what gets me every time I think about Tunguska? It's not just the raw power of that explosion, though that's mind-bending enough. It's how this single event transformed our understanding of cosmic threats while still keeping its mysteries. Trust me, I've spent countless hours in dusty archives and remote libraries piecing this puzzle together, and the more I learn, the more fascinating it becomes.

Here's what we know for sure: something massive came screaming through our atmosphere that summer morning in 1908, packed enough punch to flatten 80 million trees, and vanished without leaving so much as a calling card. The explosion was so powerful it knocked people off their feet 40 miles away and lit up skies across Europe. Think about that, bright enough to read by in London at midnight, thousands of miles from ground zero. That's not just a light show; that's a cosmic wake-up call.

The science points pretty clearly to an asteroid airburst, probably about the size of a football field, exploding several miles up in the atmosphere. But don't let that straightforward explanation fool you. We're still finding new clues in those Siberian soils, tiny glass beads with cosmic fingerprints, patterns in the devastation that challenge our computer models, and questions that keep scientists scratching their heads.

What really strikes me is how Tunguska changed us. Before 1908, the idea of cosmic objects threatening Earth was mostly science fiction fodder. Now? We've got entire organizations dedicated to tracking space rocks, international protocols for planetary defense, and an annual Asteroid Day (on June 30th, naturally) to remind us that sometimes the biggest threats come from above.

So yeah, maybe we'll never know exactly what object decided to rearrange the Siberian landscape that morning. But in a way, that lingering uncertainty makes Tunguska even more important. It reminds us that the universe still has plenty of surprises up its sleeve, and sometimes the best scientific discoveries aren't the answers we find, but the questions that keep us looking up at the stars, wondering what might come next.

Next time you're outside on a clear night, take a moment to look up at that vast cosmic ocean above us. Somewhere out there, perhaps another Tunguska-sized surprise is making its way through space. But this time, thanks to that mysterious visitor in 1908, we're at least keeping our eyes open. And maybe that's the most important legacy of all.

Chapter 8

The Mad Gasser of Mattoon

America's Strangest Crime Wave

O N A MUGGY SEPTEMBER evening in 1944, the peaceful town of Mattoon, Illinois, found itself thrust into a mystery that would baffle investigators and psychologists for decades to come. What began with a single report of a sweet-smelling gas being sprayed through a bedroom window would soon spiral into a two-week period of panic that would earn Mattoon an unusual place in American criminal history. The strange saga began with a seemingly ordinary news report in the Mattoon Daily Journal-Gazette, where Urban Raef described how he and his wife had awakened to a peculiar, sweet odor in their bedroom that left them feeling nauseous and temporarily paralyzed. Look, I've spent years cruising America's backroads, chasing down weird tales and roadside attractions, but this one? This thing that happened in Mattoon? It's the kind of story that makes you question everything you think you know about small-town life.

As more reports flooded in, the details got wilder. Folks described some shadowy figure, picture a character straight out of a noir film, skulking around in the dark, spraying this mysterious gas through windows and door cracks. The victims all told similar stories: burning throats, legs turning to jelly, and the kind of nausea that makes you swear off your aunt's holiday fruitcake forever. The really bizarre part? The police couldn't find a single shred of physical evidence. Not one fingerprint, not one empty gas canister, nothing. Just dozens of terrified residents all describing the same phantom attacker.

Now, here's where it gets really interesting. The national press caught wind of the story and had a field day with it. They dubbed our mystery menace the "Mad Gasser of Mattoon" or my personal favorite, the "Phantom Anesthetist" (sounds like a rejected comic book villain, doesn't it?). The whole town went into full panic mode, picture this: hardware stores selling out of window screens faster than hot dogs at a baseball game, neighbors setting up watch rotations like amateur commandos, and folks boarding up their windows as if a hurricane was coming. Except this storm was invisible, unpredictable, and possibly all in their heads.

I've dug through dusty police files, interviewed old-timers who remembered the panic firsthand, and even spent a few nights walking those same streets where the Gasser supposedly prowled. Let me tell you something, when you're standing on a quiet Mattoon street corner at midnight, knowing what happened there back in '44, every shadow starts looking suspicious and every weird smell makes your heart skip a beat. It's funny how fear can turn the most ordinary small town into something straight out of a thriller novel.

Whether the Mad Gasser was real or just mass hysteria fueled by wartime anxiety (and believe me, there are good arguments on both sides), one thing's for certain, this case changed Mattoon forever. It became one of those stories that gets passed down through generations, making kids check under their beds and adults double-check their window locks. The kind of tale that reminds us how the line between reality and imagination can get mighty blurry when fear takes hold of a community.

As someone who's spent countless hours mapping out America's strangest stories, I can tell you that the Mad Gasser case hits differently. Maybe it's because it happened in such an ordinary place, to such ordinary people. Or maybe it's because, deep down, we all know that the scariest mysteries aren't the ones involving ghosts or monsters, they're the ones that make us question what's real and what isn't, the ones that turn our safe, familiar world upside down when we least expect it.

The Initial Attacks and Public Response

Let me tell you about the night that kicked off Mattoon's descent into panic, because trust me, I've seen my share of small-town mysteries, but this one's a doozy. It all started with Urban and his wife[62][63], just regular folks trying to get some shut-eye in their Grant Avenue home. Now, picture this: you're sound asleep when suddenly this sickly-sweet smell hits your nostrils, and before you know it, your legs feel like they're made of concrete. Mrs. Raef tries to scream, but her throat's on fire instead. The doctors initially wrote it off as a faulty gas stove (don't you love how experts always reach for the simple explanation?), but boy, were they in for a surprise.

Word spread faster than gossip at a church picnic, and suddenly everyone had a story to tell. Take Mrs. Violet Driskell and her daughter Ramona[61], they're minding their own business when someone decides to play home decorator and removes their storm window. Next thing you know, poor Ramona's getting sick all over the place, and Mrs. Driskell swears she saw some shadowy figure pulling a vanishing act into the night. It's like something straight out of those pulp novels you'd find at a roadside gas station.

Then the floodgates really opened. The Baileys, Katherine Tuzzo, the Haskell family, they all started reporting the same weird experience[61]. Gas coming through windows, folks getting sick, legs going numb. It was like some twisted game of copycat, except nobody was having any fun. The most detailed account came from Frances Smith (she ran the Columbian Grade School) and her sister Maxine[61]. They didn't just get the usual symptoms, they heard this bizarre buzzing sound outside their window, like some kind of twisted ice cream truck from hell.

Within two weeks[62], we're talking more than two dozen official reports, with plenty more unofficial ones floating around. I've seen my share of small-town panics, but this one took the cake and the whole bakery with it. Local papers started running headlines that would make Stephen King proud[60][62]. By September 10th, things had gone full-tilt bonkers. You had farmers and townspeople playing vigilante, patrolling the streets with whatever weapons they could get their hands on. The poor police were stuck playing referee, trying to prevent these amateur crime fighters from accidentally taking each other out while also hunting for their phantom menace[61][60].

Even the FBI got in on the action[61], though they had about as much luck finding physical evidence as I've had finding a decent cup of coffee at 3 AM in rural Nebraska, which is to say, none at all. The hardware stores? They looked like Black Friday sales had hit early, with everyone scrambling to buy window screens and locks. It was like the whole town was trying to fortify itself against a ghost.

Here's where it gets really interesting though, all these victims kept describing the same thing: some mysterious figure in dark clothes, skulking around at night, spraying this paralyzing gas that would make your throat burn and your legs give out[62][63][61]. The symptoms were so consistent it was spooky. But despite having more armed patrols than a military base[61], nobody ever caught our phantom gasser.

Now, the official folks, your police types and medical professionals, eventually started leaning toward the mass hysteria explanation[62]. They talked about anxiety and environmental odors, trying to make sense of it all with nice, neat scientific explanations. But let me tell you something, when you've got this many people all describing the same extremely specific symptoms[63][62], it makes you wonder. Maybe sometimes the truth is stranger than any explanation we can come up with. That's what keeps me driving these backroads, collecting these stories, because you never know when you might stumble across another Mattoon, another moment when reality decides to take a vacation and leave us all scratching our heads.

Mass Hysteria vs. Real Threat: The Police Investigation

Let me tell you something I've learned from years of chasing down bizarre stories across America's heartland, sometimes the line between reality and mass panic is about as clear as a foggy night in the Smoky Mountains. When it comes to the Mattoon investigation, boy, did the local police have their hands full trying to figure out which side of that line they were dealing with[62 61 64].

Now, Chief of Police C.E. Cole didn't mess around. He had his officers hitting the streets like they were trying to win a scavenger hunt, ramping up night patrols and encouraging folks to keep watch like suburban commandos[60]. But here's where things get interesting, on September 5th, they actually found something concrete: a suspicious white cloth that smelled funky, along with a skeleton key and lipstick tube at the Cordes family home. When Mrs. Beulah Cordes got a whiff of that cloth, she ended up with facial swelling and nausea that lasted a couple hours[61]. Finally, some real evidence! Or so they thought.

But hold onto your detective hats, because this is where the case starts twisting like a mountain road. The state boys and even the FBI joined the party[64 60], and they noticed something peculiar, in most cases, only one person in a household would get sick while everyone else was fine[64]. It's like having a ghost that only appears to one person at a time. The investigators started wondering if they were chasing their tails, looking at everything from factory fumes to spilled cleaning supplies[62].

I've spent enough time poking around small-town mysteries to know that sometimes the simplest explanation isn't always the right one. But despite throwing everything but the kitchen sink at this investigation, extra officers, extensive searches, the works, they couldn't nail down a suspect. That stuff from the Cordes' porch? That was their one and only piece of physical evidence[60]. Talk about trying to solve a puzzle with most of the pieces missing!

As September wore on, the police found themselves in a pickle that would make even Sherlock Holmes scratch his head. The more they dug into it, the more they started leaning toward the mass hysteria theory[62 61 64 60]. I mean, think about it, this was 1944, everyone was jumpy about the war, and the newspapers were having a field day with the story. But here's the kicker, they couldn't completely rule out a real attacker either. Not with that physical evidence from the Cordes incident and all those victims describing the same symptoms: burning sensations, temporary paralysis, and nausea that would make a carnival ride seem tame[61 63].

From my experience driving these backroads and collecting strange tales, I can tell you that the Mattoon case sits in that twilight zone between explained and unexplained. Kind of like those roadside attractions that look completely different depending on which angle you're viewing them from. While most experts these days tip their hats toward the mass hysteria explanation[62], there's still something about those consistent symptoms and that one piece of physical evidence that makes you wonder. Could there have been something more concrete stalking the streets of Mattoon during those tense September nights? Maybe that's why this case still fascinates us, it reminds us that sometimes the most intriguing mysteries are the ones that don't fit neatly into any box we try to put them in.

Social Impact and Historical Legacy

You know what fascinates me most about the Mad Gasser incident? It's not just the mystery itself, it's how it transformed Mattoon from your typical Midwest town into a living laboratory of human behavior. I've crisscrossed this country enough times to know that small towns have their own kind of magic, but Mattoon in '44? That was something else entirely.

Let me paint you a picture: Hardware stores stripped bare of window locks and screens faster than a tornado through a trailer park. Neighbors who'd barely exchanged hellos suddenly forming armed patrols[61], turning their quiet streets into something out of a wartime newsreel. The whole social fabric of the town got rewoven practically overnight, and not necessarily for the better. You had folks side-eyeing their neighbors, jumping at shadows, and treating every unfamiliar face like a potential gasser[62].

But here's where it gets really interesting, the *Mattoon Daily Journal-Gazette* found itself caught in a wild dance between reporting the news and accidentally feeding the frenzy[62]. With each new headline, each fresh report, the paper was simultaneously informing and inflaming. I've seen my share of small-town papers, but this was like watching a feedback loop gone haywire. The more they reported, the more reports came in, and round and round it went[66].

Now, I spend a lot of time in off-the-beaten-path museums and local historical societies, and let me tell you, the Mad Gasser case has become catnip for academics studying mass behavior[62][66]. They love picking apart how a community can basically create its own reality. Think about it: all these folks reporting similar symptoms, burning sensations, temporary paralysis, nausea, with barely any physical evidence to back it up[62]. Except for that one weird incident at the Cordes place, where they actually found something concrete.

But here's what really gets my gears turning, this wasn't just about mass hysteria versus real threat. The whole episode revealed something deeper about how communities respond to crises. You had this perfect storm of wartime anxiety, media coverage, and good old-fashioned fear of the unknown[66]. Sound familiar? It should, because we're still seeing these patterns play out today, just with different bogeymen and faster news cycles.

And let's talk about lasting impact, shall we? The Mad Gasser didn't just vanish into history like some roadside attraction that's seen better days. This incident became a cornerstone case study in how communities handle unexplained threats[62][66]. Every time I visit Mattoon (and yes, I've made the pilgrimage more than once), I find locals who can still tell you exactly where their grandparents were during the panic, what windows they boarded up, what streets they avoided.

The beauty of the Mad Gasser case, if you can call it that, is how it refuses to sit quietly in any one box. Was it mass hysteria? Maybe. A real attacker? Possibly. The truth probably lies somewhere in that murky middle ground where reality and perception do their strange dance[66]. And isn't that just the perfect metaphor for how communities deal with fear and uncertainty?

In my travels across America's backroads, I've seen plenty of towns with their own strange tales, but Mattoon's story strikes a different chord. It reminds us that sometimes the most powerful forces shaping our communities aren't the things we can see or touch, they're the invisible currents of fear, trust, and collective belief that run beneath the surface of every small town, just waiting for something to stir them up. You know what keeps me up at night about the Mad Gasser case? It's not the mystery itself, though that's plenty intriguing. It's how this whole incident peels back the curtain on what happens when fear and uncertainty creep into a small town's DNA.

I've spent years documenting America's strangest stories, and let me tell you, there's something uniquely unsettling about what happened in Mattoon. The physical evidence from the Cordes family home sits like a stubborn puzzle piece that won't quite fit into the mass hysteria theory. That white cloth with its strange chemical smell produced real, documented symptoms. Yet the pattern of attacks, where often only one person in a household would experience symptoms while others slept peacefully, points to something more complex than a simple gas-wielding prowler.

But here's what really gets me: the way this case reveals how communities process the unexplainable. The hardware stores emptying of window locks, neighbors forming amateur patrol groups, the police caught between protecting people from a possible threat and preventing panic-induced accidents, it's like watching a masterclass in collective fear response. The local paper found itself walking that razor's edge between informing the public and potentially feeding the frenzy.

Modern research, like Theodore Martinez's fascinating work mapping the attacks along old trolley routes, shows how these historical mysteries keep evolving. Fresh eyes find new patterns, challenge old assumptions, and remind us that sometimes the most intriguing stories are hiding right under our noses, in places we pass every day without a second glance.

In my travels across America's backroads and byways, I've realized that the best mysteries aren't always about finding definitive answers. Sometimes they're about understanding how communities react when faced with the unexplainable, how fear can transform ordinary streets into something alien and threatening, and how the ripples of these strange events can echo through generations. The Mad Gasser of Mattoon might remain forever in that foggy space between mass hysteria and genuine threat, but maybe that's exactly where this story belongs, reminding us that reality isn't always as clear-cut as we'd like it to be.

Chapter 9

The Poison Squad
When Government Workers Ate Toxins for Science

I N 1902, A PECULIAR advertisement appeared in Washington D.C., seeking young, healthy men willing to be poisoned in the name of science. This wasn't some mad scientist's scheme, but rather a government-sanctioned experiment that would revolutionize food safety in America. These brave souls, dubbed "The Poison Squad" by the press, weren't trying to win a bizarre eating contest or chasing viral fame, they were part of a groundbreaking government experiment that would fundamentally change what ends up on our dinner plates. Picture this: every morning, these volunteers would stroll into a specially designed dining room in the basement of the USDA building, knowing full well they were about to chow down on foods laced with everything from borax to formaldehyde. Talk about a breakfast of champions!

Now, I've eaten some questionable gas station hot dogs in my cross-country travels, but nothing compared to what these folks voluntarily signed up for. Think about it, these government clerks would sit down to seemingly normal meals: fresh bread, wholesome milk, hearty stews. The twist? Each dish came with a side of carefully measured industrial chemicals that would make a modern food safety inspector faint. The real kicker? They kept coming back, meal after meal, even as their bodies rebelled with everything from violent nausea to temporary paralysis.

The mastermind behind this wild experiment was Dr. Harvey Washington Wiley, who I like to think of as the mad scientist of food safety (but you know, in a good way). He wasn't some cackling villain forcing people to eat poison, he was actually trying to prove just how dangerous these common food additives were. Back then, food manufacturers could basically throw whatever chemicals they wanted into food without telling anyone. Formaldehyde in milk? Sure! Borax in your butter? Why not! It was like the Wild West of food preservation, minus the cool cowboy hats.

When word got out about these experiments, newspapers had a field day. I mean, government workers voluntarily eating poison? That's headline gold! They started calling the volunteers "The Poison Squad," which honestly sounds more like a rejected superhero team name than a scientific study group. But here's the thing, these everyday heroes were actually changing history one queasy bite at a time. Their suffering led directly to the Pure Food and Drug Act of 1906, America's first real food safety law.

The next time you check a food label or feel confident that your breakfast won't include a side of borax, thank these gastrointestinal gladiators. And hey, maybe think twice before complaining about your cafeteria food, at least it's not intentionally poisoned in the name of science.

The Birth of Food Safety Testing: Dr. Wiley's Revolutionary Approach

You know what's really wild? In 1902, while most government scientists were doing whatever boring stuff government scientists usually did, Dr. Harvey Washington Wiley was basically running a real-life science experiment that would make today's ethics boards have a collective meltdown. He turned the USDA's basement into what newspapers dubbed the world's most dangerous dining room, complete with a side of potentially lethal preservatives[67][68].

Picture this: twelve young men, mostly USDA employees with iron stomachs and brass nerves, volunteering to systematically poison themselves. Not for fame or fortune, mind you, but for the noble cause of proving that maybe, just maybe, we shouldn't be putting industrial chemicals in our food. These brave souls would gather three times daily in a clean, well-lit basement room that looked more like a respectable restaurant than a mad scientist's lab. The menu? Standard American fare with a twist, a dash of borax here, a sprinkle of formaldehyde there, you know, the usual stuff food manufacturers were sneaking into everything from milk to meat[69].

The whole thing was run like a bizarre cooking show meets scientific study. Half the group would get meals spiked with the chemical of the month, while the other half got to enjoy their food without extra "seasoning." Then they'd switch, because fair is fair when you're voluntarily consuming questionable substances. The volunteers went through regular medical check-ups and had to keep detailed records of their symptoms. It was like a food diary from hell, but it was actually the first controlled experimental testing of commercial food additives in American history[67][68].

Now, I've had some questionable meals at roadside diners across this great nation, but nothing compared to what these guys endured. We're talking severe stomach pain, nausea, vomiting, and even temporary paralysis. Yet these absolute champions kept showing up for more. That's dedication that makes my commitment to finding America's best truck stop coffee look pretty wimpy in comparison[67][68].

Wiley wasn't just running a scientific experiment, he was staging a public relations coup. He knew that cold, hard data alone wouldn't cut it. He needed the public's attention, and boy did he get it. The newspapers ate up the story (pun absolutely intended), dubbing his volunteers the "Poison Squad." The publicity helped unite an unlikely alliance of women's groups, consumer advocates, and even honest manufacturers who were tired of competing with companies willing to poison their customers to save a buck[67].

The impact was dramatic. Four of the preservatives tested by the Poison Squad were quickly abandoned by manufacturers[71]. But the real victory came in 1906 with the Pure Food and Drug Act, America's first comprehensive food safety law. It was like someone finally turned on the lights in a very dark kitchen, and a lot of unsavory practices scurried away like roaches[70].

Every time I check a food label today (which, let's be honest, is usually after I've already eaten something questionable), I think about those brave souls in that USDA basement. They literally put their health on the line to prove that maybe, just maybe, we shouldn't be preserving our food with the same stuff used to embalm bodies. Talk about taking one for the team, or in this case, taking several thousand questionable bites for the entire nation[67][68].

Common Food Additives and Their Hidden Dangers in the 1900s

You think your grandmother's cooking was all wholesome ingredients and old-fashioned goodness? Well, pull up a chair, because I'm about to serve you a disturbing slice of early 1900s food history that'll make you grateful for modern regulations. Back then, food manufacturers weren't just playing fast and loose with safety, they were practically running a chemistry experiment in America's kitchens.

Let me paint you a picture of your average 1900s pantry: That appetizing green candy? Probably colored with copper arsenite, which is exactly as poisonous as it sounds[73]. That lovely rosy cheese? Thank red lead for that festive hue, you know, the same stuff that causes brain damage[73]. And that butter staying mysteriously fresh in the summer heat? That's our old friend borax at work, yes, the same stuff we now use to kill roaches. Bon appétit!

Now, let's talk about milk, that wholesome symbol of health and vitality. Except in the early 1900s, it was more like a chemistry experiment gone wrong. Dairy producers were playing mad scientist, adding formaldehyde to prevent spoilage[72]. They called it "embalmed milk," which is probably the most honest food labeling of the era. Think about that, people were literally drinking the same stuff used to preserve dead bodies. And here I thought gas station sushi was risky!

But wait, there's more! Those vibrantly colored candies and beverages? They got their eye-catching hues from coal tar dyes, which we later discovered were carcinogenic[73]. Salicylic acid, which could tear up your insides, was casually tossed into canned vegetables like seasoning[72]. And manufacturers didn't even bother listing these ingredients, they considered them "trade secrets." Because apparently, the secret ingredient was poison.

The really wild part? Most of these additives weren't sneaked in by some shadowy food conspiracy, they were openly praised as modern miracles of food preservation! Borax and boric acid were the superstars of the preservative world, used in everything from meat to dairy. Sure, they caused nausea, vomiting, and kidney damage, but hey, at least your butter didn't spoil, right?[72]

Here's a fun fact that'll make you appreciate modern food labels: When saccharin first hit the scene as an artificial sweetener, it went through more plot twists than a soap opera, repeatedly banned and reinstated as new health concerns popped up[73]. It's like the food industry was playing a game of "Will This Kill You?" with the American public.

Thankfully, this chemical free-for-all started to wind down with the Pure Food and Drug Act of 1906[72]. For the first time, manufacturers actually had to list preservatives on their labels and, here's the crazy part, prove they were safe before dumping them into our food[75]. Revolutionary concept, right?

So next time you're reading a food label and rolling your eyes at all those long chemical names, remember this: at least they're required to tell you what's in there. And more importantly, someone had to prove it won't kill you before they could add it to your food. We've come a long way from the days when "breakfast of champions" might literally include champion-grade embalming fluid.

From Poison Squad to Pure Food Act: The Legacy of Human Testing

If you think getting legislation passed today is tough, imagine trying to convince Congress that food companies shouldn't be allowed to casually poison their customers. That's exactly what Dr. Wiley and his brave band of government guinea pigs managed to pull off, turning their queasy stomachs into lasting change for American food safety.

By 1906, the Poison Squad experiments had become front-page news across the country. Newspapers couldn't get enough of these "human guinea pigs" who were deliberately eating their way through a chemical menu to prove a point. The public was equal parts horrified and fascinated, kind of like watching a train wreck, if the train was full of formaldehyde-laced milk and borax-seasoned butter[76].

Here's where things get interesting: all this publicity actually worked! When the Pure Food and Drug Act finally landed on President Theodore Roosevelt's desk in 1906, it wasn't just another boring piece of legislation, it was the culmination of years of strategic nausea and very public indigestion. For the first time ever, food manufacturers had to actually list their chemical additives on labels (shocking, I know) and prove they were safe before using them. It's like someone finally turned on the lights at a really sketchy restaurant[76].

But here's my favorite part: this law laid the groundwork for what would become the Food and Drug Administration (FDA). Think about that, every time you read a food label or feel confident your milk won't pickle your insides, you're basically experiencing the ripple effects of some very queasy government workers from over a century ago[76].

The real genius of the Poison Squad wasn't just in proving these additives were dangerous, it was in making the public care about food safety in the first place. Dr. Wiley understood something fundamental about human nature: people might ignore statistics, but they can't look away from a good story. And what better story than voluntary government workers turning their stomachs into testing grounds for the greater good?

Today's food safety testing looks a lot different (thankfully). We've traded human guinea pigs for sophisticated lab equipment and animal studies. But every food recall, every ingredient label, and every FDA inspection carries a little bit of the Poison Squad's

DNA. These brave souls basically ate their way through a chemical nightmare so future generations wouldn't have to.

Next time you're grocery shopping and checking labels (you do check labels, right?), spare a thought for those iron-stomached heroes who made it possible. They turned their digestive distress into a legacy that's still protecting us today. Now that's what I call a gut reaction to injustice! You know, sitting here in my favorite roadside diner, sipping what the menu optimistically calls "coffee," I can't help but marvel at how far we've come in food safety. Those Poison Squad volunteers weren't just government workers with iron stomachs, they were pioneers who literally put their lives on the line to change how America thinks about food safety.

Their experiments might seem bizarre by today's standards, but they fundamentally shifted how we approach food regulation. Think about it: before these brave souls started systematically poisoning themselves, manufacturers could dump whatever chemicals they wanted into our food without even telling us. It was like playing Russian roulette with your breakfast cereal.

Looking at the evidence, it's clear their strategy was brilliant in its simplicity. Instead of just compiling dry statistics, Dr. Wiley created a compelling narrative that grabbed public attention. Every queasy stomach, every bout of nausea, every detailed medical report built an irrefutable case that these common food additives weren't just questionable, they were downright dangerous.

But here's what really gets me: these weren't some specially trained lab technicians or desperate volunteers looking for quick cash. These were ordinary government clerks who showed up day after day, knowing they were about to eat things that would make them sick, all because they believed in making food safer for everyone. That's not just dedication, that's heroism served with a side of formaldehyde.

The impact of their sacrifice rippled far beyond their immediate discomfort. Each poisoned meal helped build the foundation for modern food safety regulations. Their collective indigestion led directly to the Pure Food and Drug Act of 1906, which finally put some actual teeth into food safety enforcement. Every ingredient label you read today, every FDA inspection that happens, every recall of dangerous products, it all traces back to those twelve brave souls in that USDA basement.

So next time you're checking a food label or confidently biting into a sandwich without worrying about borax content, spare a thought for the Poison Squad. They turned their stomachs into testing grounds so we wouldn't have to. Now if you'll excuse me, I need to ask the waitress what exactly makes this coffee "special", old habits die hard!

Chapter 10

The Ghost Army

How Inflatable Tanks Won World War II

I N THE SPRING OF 1944, while real battles raged across Europe, a peculiar army
unit was busy inflating rubber tanks and playing recorded sound effects of military
movements through powerful speakers. The 23rd Headquarters Special Troops, a clas-
sified unit of the U.S. Army, would become one of World War II's most unusual yet
effective weapons, an army of illusion that helped win the war without firing a single shot.
The Ghost Army of WWII was perhaps history's most creative military unit, employing
Hollywood-style deception on a grand scale to help secure victory for the Allies. Think

of it as the world's biggest magic show, where the audience was the German military and the stakes were literally life and death. While most soldiers were loading real ammo, these creative commandos were inflating rubber tanks that looked so real they could fool aerial photography. I've seen photos of these things, they're like those giant balloon characters from the Macy's Parade, except instead of Snoopy, you've got a Sherman tank that could pass for real from a thousand feet up.

But here's the kicker, the visual tricks were just the opening act. These folks had a whole sound effects department that would put modern Hollywood to shame. They'd roll out these massive speakers (and I mean massive, like "wake-the-dead" massive) and play carefully orchestrated soundtracks of army life. Tanks rumbling, troops marching, mechanics working, all recorded and mixed with the precision of a hit record. You could hear these audio illusions from fifteen miles away! Imagine trying to sleep while your neighbor's party music shakes your windows, now imagine that party music is actually the sound of an entire army division on the move.

The real genius was in the details though. These weren't just some theater kids playing dress-up, they created entire fictional military units complete with their own patches, vehicle markings, and radio chatter. They were basically running a Broadway show, except instead of singing and dancing, they were convincing enemy intelligence that phantom armies were marching across Europe. And they were good at it too, so good that they successfully impersonated more than 20 different U.S. Army units during their secret operations.

Think about that for a minute, a bunch of artists, sound engineers, and creative types basically turned warfare into performance art. And it worked! Their deceptions are estimated to have saved thousands of Allied lives by drawing enemy attention away from actual military units and thoroughly confusing German intelligence about Allied positions and strength. The whole operation was kept under wraps for over 40 years after the war ended, talk about a long-running show! Only in the 1990s did we finally get to peek behind the curtain and see just how these creative warriors helped win the war with rubber, speakers, and pure imagination.

Tactical Deception: The Art of Military Illusion

Now, you might think having an army of just over 1,000 people pretending to be 30,000 would be about as effective as trying to convince your mom that your little brother ate all the cookies, but these folks were masters of misdirection. They were like that friend who can make you look at their right hand while their left is snagging the last slice of pizza, except instead of pizza, they were protecting actual armies.

The really wild part? This wasn't just some desperate last-ditch effort, this was carefully planned theatrical warfare. The Ghost Army recruited artists, engineers, and advertising pros who could think creatively under pressure. We're talking future fashion designer Bill Blass and painter Ellsworth Kelly[78][79] mixing it up with sound engineers and radio operators. These weren't your average GI Joes, with an average IQ of 119, they were more likely to quote Shakespeare than Patton[78].

Let me paint you a picture of how these elaborate deceptions worked. Picture a field in France, where in just 20 minutes (about the time it takes to get a pizza delivered), this crew could set up an entire fake tank battalion[77][79]. These weren't just balloon animals at a kid's party, these inflatable tanks were so detailed they could fool German reconnaissance planes from thousands of feet up[77]. Meanwhile, the sound team would be setting up their greatest hits album of warfare, tank engines revving, troops shouting, construction equipment clanking, all carefully choreographed to convince anyone listening that they were hearing the real deal[78].

During Operation Bettembourg, one of their greatest performances, they pulled off something that would make David Copperfield jealous. Using nothing but rubber props and sound effects, they convinced German commanders that a major attack was coming in what was actually a quiet sector[80]. It was like convincing your cat the red dot is real, except instead of a cat, it was the entire German military intelligence apparatus.

Think about the nerves it took to pull this off. As Captain Fred Fox noted, "Officers who had once commanded 32-ton tanks felt frustrated and helpless with a battalion of rubber M-4s, 93 pounds fully inflated. The adjustment from man of action to man of wile was most difficult."[77] It was like asking a boxer to win a fight by shadow puppetry, it required a complete mental shift in how to approach warfare.

The Ghost Army's work was so hush-hush that even after the war ended, they had to keep quiet about their contributions. It wasn't until the 1990s that their story was declassified, and they had to wait until 2024 to receive the Congressional Gold Medal[81]. Talk about a delayed standing ovation! But here's the thing, their techniques changed how we think about modern military deception[79]. They proved that sometimes the most powerful weapon isn't the one that goes boom, but the one that makes the enemy think they heard a boom from fifteen miles away.

And you know what's really fascinating? These master illusionists managed to create phantom armies that helped drive the Germans absolutely bonkers trying to figure out where the real Allied forces were. It's like they were running a continental-scale shell game, except instead of hiding a pea, they were hiding entire army divisions. They created such convincing deceptions that German intelligence reports from the time read like they were written by someone who'd had one too many schnapps trying to track down armies that existed only in their imagination.

Sound and Fury: Audio Engineering in Warfare

You know how some folks can set an entire mood just by playing the right song? Well, the Ghost Army took that concept and cranked it up to eleven, literally. They weren't just playing music; they were orchestrating the soundtrack of war with speakers that could shake the ground from miles away.

Let me tell you about these audio wizards and their absolutely bonkers sound system. Picture the biggest, beefiest speakers you've ever seen at a rock concert, then imagine them mounted on military trucks and capable of projecting sound for fifteen miles[83]. These weren't your typical boom boxes, we're talking about quarter-ton speakers that could convince enemy troops they were hearing an entire armored division rolling through their backyard.

The real genius was in the mixing. These sound engineers were basically the world's first military DJs, but instead of mixing beats, they were layering recordings of tank movements, soldier conversations, and construction equipment. They'd record these sounds onto massive spools of wire, think old-school tape, but way more hardcore, that could stretch up to two miles long[83]. It's like they were formulating the world's most intense podcast, except their target audience was the German army.

You might be wondering where all this audio tech came from. Well, it turns out the military had been playing around with sound since World War I, when they first started using acoustic defense systems to track enemy positions. Teams of soldiers would huddle together, listening intently to battlefield sounds like prehistoric radar operators[84]. By WWII, they'd developed all sorts of fancy gear, like the T-30 throat microphone that could pick up a whisper even in the chaos of combat[82].

But here's where it gets really interesting, remember Shure, the company that probably made your favorite microphone? During the war, they were cranking out hundreds of thousands of specialized military mics[82]. These weren't just for the Ghost Army's sonic deceptions; they were being used in everything from hospital rooms to training facilities. The work was so crucial that Shure actually told their employees not to enlist, apparently, making microphones was considered more important than carrying a rifle[82].

What makes this whole operation even more remarkable is who they recruited to run it. Instead of traditional soldiers, they brought in musicians, sound engineers, and other creative types who knew their way around audio equipment. These folks weren't trained for combat, they were trained to make hit records and radio shows. But in the middle of the biggest war in history, they proved that sometimes the most effective weapon isn't a gun or a bomb, but a perfectly timed sound effect.

The impact of their work didn't stop when the war ended either. All those audio tricks they pioneered? They ended up influencing military deception techniques for decades[85]. Plus, a lot of the technology they developed for portable recording and playback equipment helped shape the future of commercial audio engineering. It's kind of wild to think that some of the tech that went into fooling Nazi forces might have indirectly influenced the equipment used to record your favorite albums.

So next time you're blasting music through your speakers, remember the Ghost Army's sound team. They proved that with enough creativity and the right equipment, you can convince anyone to hear exactly what you want them to, even if what they're hearing isn't really there at all.

The Artists Who Went to War: Creative Minds in Military Service

Picture this, while most folks were honing their aim with rifles, a special group of soldiers was perfecting their brush strokes and mixing paint colors. I'm not talking about some military art therapy program here, these were full-fledged combat artists who turned their creative talents into secret weapons. And let me tell you, they made MacGyver look like an amateur!

Now, you might be wondering how exactly an art degree helps win a war. Well, turns out those years of figure drawing and color theory came in pretty handy when you needed to make a plywood tank look real enough to fool enemy pilots flying overhead. These weren't just any artists, we're talking about graduates from places like Rhode Island School of Design and the Art Institute of Chicago[86]. They brought the same attention to detail to military deception that they'd previously used to paint still lifes of fruit bowls.

Take the French military's Camoufleurs during World War I, these folks were basically the original masters of hide and seek[86]. They turned battlefield concealment into an art form, quite literally. Using their understanding of color, shadow, and perspective, they could make entire artillery positions disappear like magic. It's like they were playing a high-stakes game of "Where's Waldo?" except instead of finding Waldo, the goal was making sure nobody could find your army.

But here's where it gets really interesting, these artist-soldiers weren't just painting things to look like other things. They were creating entire fictional military units complete with their own distinctive looks and personalities. Think of it as method acting, but with tanks and troops instead of stage props and costumes. Ellsworth Kelly, who would later become a famous minimalist painter, spent his war years working on these deceptions. He once said, "We used our skills to save lives, to fool the enemy, and to contribute to the war in a way only artists could."[86]

Some artists took their wartime roles to extreme lengths. Frank Fujita Jr., while stuck in a Japanese POW camp, secretly kept a diary filled with sketches documenting camp life and torture[87]. Talk about dedication to your art, he risked death to create these historical records! Meanwhile, artists like Robert Benney were out in the Pacific Theater, sketching medical procedures and battlefield scenes that cameras couldn't or wouldn't capture[87].

The real genius of these creative warriors wasn't just in their technical skills, it was in their ability to think differently. When most military planners were thinking about firepower and troop movements, these artists were considering things like shadow length and color harmony. They proved that sometimes the best way to win a battle isn't by fighting it head-on, but by making the enemy see exactly what you want them to see.

Here's a mind-bending fact: during World War II, the U.S. Army's 23rd Headquarters Special Troops staged more than 20 major deception operations[88]. Each one was like a massive art installation, except instead of being displayed in a gallery, it was staged on the battlefields of Europe. And the critics? Well, let's just say the German high command gave them some pretty convincing reviews, they fell for these deceptions hook, line, and sinker.

As one artist from the Cleveland Institute of Art put it, "We painted, we built, we staged. We were actors and artists, and our canvas was the battlefield."[88] Talk about a unique portfolio! These folks weren't just making art, they were using their creative skills to save lives and change the course of history. Now that's what I call applied arts! You know what really gets me about the Ghost Army? It's not just that they pulled off some of the greatest military deceptions in history, it's that they did it with rubber tanks, sound effects, and pure imagination. These folks weren't your typical soldiers; they were artists, actors, and sound engineers who turned warfare into the world's most high-stakes theater production.

The evidence of their success is pretty mind-blowing when you dig into it. They staged over 20 major deceptions, fooled German intelligence repeatedly, and saved countless lives without firing a shot. But they weren't just good at tricking the enemy, they revolutionized how we think about military deception. The Ghost Army proved that sometimes the most effective weapon isn't the biggest gun, but the most convincing illusion.

Here's the really wild part, after spending years creating phantom armies that never existed, these creative warriors had to pretend that their own incredible achievements didn't exist either. For over four decades, they couldn't even tell their families about what they'd done. Talk about a tough audience! When their story was finally declassified in the 1990s, it revealed something pretty profound about warfare and creativity, that sometimes the best way to win isn't by being the strongest, but by being the smartest and most imaginative.

The Ghost Army's legacy lives on in modern military operations, where deception and psychological warfare are still crucial tools. But I think their real lesson goes beyond military strategy. They showed us that creativity, when properly applied, can be more powerful than brute force. That artists, actors, and dreamers can sometimes accomplish what traditional soldiers can't. And that sometimes, the best way to change the world isn't by destroying things, but by making people believe in things that aren't really there.

Next time you're at a concert, getting blown away by massive speakers, or watching inflatable decorations bob around during the holidays, remember the Ghost Army. They took those same basic elements, sound, air, and imagination, and used them to help win the biggest war in history. Now that's what I call a command performance!

Conclusion

I N SUM, HISTORY HAS a remarkable way of defying our expectations, revealing stories that challenge what we think we know about the past. From the inexplicable Dancing Plague of 1518 to the strategic deceptions of the Ghost Army in World War II, these ten historical mysteries remind us that truth can indeed be stranger than fiction.

Through these extraordinary tales, we've witnessed how seemingly impossible events shaped our world in unexpected ways. The Great Molasses Flood led to crucial industrial safety reforms. The Poison Squad's voluntary consumption of toxic substances paved the way for modern food safety regulations. Even the peculiar case of the Mad Gasser of Mattoon taught valuable lessons about mass hysteria and community response to crisis.

These stories serve as more than mere historical curiosities, they offer profound insights into human nature, scientific inquiry, and societal development. The mystery of the Devil's Footprints demonstrates how communities grapple with the unexplainable. The Tunguska Event continues to drive scientific investigation and asteroid defense planning. The Lost Roman Legion's potential journey to ancient China reveals how interconnected our world has always been.

Perhaps most importantly, these historical mysteries remind us that our understanding of the past is constantly evolving. Whether examining the scientific evidence that debunks the Phantom Time Hypothesis or contemplating the innovative tactics of the Ghost Army, we see how historical investigation combines rigorous research with creative thinking to unlock the secrets of our past.

As we close this journey through history's most puzzling events, we're left with a deeper appreciation for the complexity of human experience. These stories challenge us to keep questioning, exploring, and remaining open to the possibility that there are still countless mysteries waiting to be discovered in the annals of history. After all, the most valuable lesson these ten historical mysteries teach us is that the past will never cease to amaze, inspire, and occasionally bewilder those who dare to explore its depths.

Endnotes

References

1 History Skills. (2024). *What caused the deadly 'dancing plague' of 1518?*. History Skills.

2 Waller, John. (2009, February). *Dancing plague of 1518*. Wikipedia.

3 Bauer, P.. (2025, July 17). *dancing plague of 1518*. Encyclopedia Britannica.

4 Kotok, A.. (2025, July 05). *Dance, Dance 'til You're Dead: The Dancing Plague of 1518*. The Science Survey.

5 Pennant-Rea N.. (2018, July 10). *The Dancing Plague of 1518*. The Public Domain Review.

6 Gargiulo, M.. (2024, February 09). *The Dancing Plague of 1518*. Michele Gargiulo.

7 Davis, M.. (2023, July). *The bizarre story of the deadly "dancing plague" of 1518*. Big Think.

8 Wikipedia contributors. (2025, July 9). *Great Molasses Flood*. Wikipedia.

9 Sharp, N.. (2016, November 19). *New Research on the Fluid Dynamics of the Boston Molasses Flood*. Improbable Research.

10 American Physical Society. (2017, January 01). *Join your Society*. American Physical Society.

[11] Archives and Records Management. (2019, January 15). *100 years ago today: Molasses crashes through Boston's North End*. Boston.gov.

[12] Tuttle A.. (2019, December). *The 1919 Molasses Flood*. Old North Church & Historic Site.

[13] Cavanaugh, R.. (2019, January 14). *The Great Molasses Flood of 1919 Was Boston's Strangest Disaster*. TIME.

[14] Massachusetts Historical Society. (2019, January 31). *The Great Molasses Flood Revisited*. Massachusetts Historical Society.

[15] Keller, J.. (2019, January 07). *How the Boston Molasses Disaster Ushered in the Era of Modern Regulation*. Pacific Standard.

[16] WeHistory.org. (2019, January 16). *Preventing Another Boston Molasses Disaster*. We History.org.

[17] Dash, Mike. (1994). *Devil's Footprints*. Wikipedia.

[18] Ian. (2008, July 26). *The Devil's Footprints*. Mysterious Britain.

[19] Moore, P.. (2015, February 09). *The Curious Case of the Devil's Foot-Prints (or the Great Devon Mystery of 1855)*. Peter Moore.

[20] Gathertales. (2023, October 15). *The Tale of the Devil's Footprints*. Gathertales.

[21] Lawrance, R.. (2022, February 22). *The Devil's Footprints*. Your Mag.

[22] Jeffers, R.. (2014, September 24). *Victorian Folklore Legend: Spring-Heeled Jack*. Every Woman Dreams.

[23] Digital Commons. (2023, December 12). *Access Denied, WAF Rule Reached*. Liberty University Digital Commons.

[24] VinePair Staff. (2024, June 12). *The Gross, Gory Mystery of the Kentucky Meat Shower*. VinePair.

[25] Pfeifle, T.. (2016, July 17). *The Great Kentucky Meat Shower*. Astonishing Legends.

[26] Wikipedia Contributors. (2024, February 14). *Kentucky meat shower*. Wikipedia.

[27] Akomolafe, D.. (2023, February 15). *The Kentucky Meat Shower: A Bizarre Phenomenon of 1876*. Vocal Media.

[28] Mental Floss Staff. (2024). *Digging Into the Explosive Mystery Behind the Kentucky Meat Shower of 1876*. Mental Floss.

[29] Cecil, C. J.. (2020, September 25). *Wonders of the World: Kentucky Meat Shower*. The Georgetonian.

[30] Randle, K.. (2025, March 02). *Bath County celebrates KY Meat Shower 149th anniversary*. LEX18.

[31] TOI Lifestyle Desk. (2024, December 31). *The bizarre Kentucky meat shower of 1876: When meat rained from the sky!*. Times of India.

[32] Roman Empire Staff. (2024, March). *The Battle of Carrhae*. Roman Empire.

[33] DailyHistory.org. (2023, October 15). *What was the impact of the Battle of Carrhae (53BC) on Rome*. DailyHistory.org.

[34] Wikipedia contributors. (2024, February 21). *Battle of Carrhae*. Wikipedia.

[35] History Hit. (2020, March 01). *The Battle of Carrhae: How Rome's Richest Man Met His End*. History Hit.

[36] Strom, C.. (2018, November 19). *The Lost Legion of Carrhae: Did a Roman Legion End Up in China?*. Ancient Origins.

[37] Wikipedia contributors. (2024, January 15). *Liqian*. Wikipedia.

[38] Lambert, P.. (2011, September 14). *Part 1 : A lost Roman legion....in China?*. HeritageDaily.

[39] Tastes of History. (2023, January 1). *Dispelling Some Myths: Romans in China*. Tastes of History.

[40] Heritage of Japan. (2010, November 24). *Silk Road Caucasian trader or Roman legion legacies?*. Heritage of Japan.

[41] Zhang Z.. (2024, November 9). *Scholars debunk myth of Roman settlement in China after DNA tests, doubt still draws tourists*. South China Morning Post.

[42] Chu, H.. (2000, August 24). *Digging for Romans in China*. Los Angeles Times.

[43] Aly, A.. (2023, May 15). *The Phantom Time Hypothesis: Did the Middle Ages Never Happen?*. Vocal Media.

[44] Wikipedia contributors. (2024, January 14). *Phantom time conspiracy theory*. Wikipedia.

[45] Mitchell, R.. (2023, August 1). *Phantom Time Theory: Did we Invent 300 Years of History?*. Historic Mysteries.

[46] Serena, K.. (2017). *Bizarre Phantom Time Hypothesis Theory Says It's Actually The Year 1720 Because The Early Middle Ages Were Faked*. The Archaeologist.

[47] Hinton, K.. (2024, April 19). *The "phantom time hypothesis" claims 297 years of history never happened*. History Facts.

[48] Grigoli L. R.. (2023, October 18). *The Bizarre (and Blatantly False) Conspiracy Theory That Says the Middle Ages Never Happened*. Mental Floss.

[49] Medievalists.net. (2020, April 10). *Why the Phantom Time Hypothesis is Wrong*. Medievalists.net.

[50] Plackett, B.. (2023, October 4). *What Is the Truth Behind the Controversial Phantom Time Hypothesis?*. Discover Magazine.

[51] Wikipedia contributors. (2024, January 18). *Tunguska event*. Wikipedia.

[52] Ol'khovatov A.. (2023, October 23). *The 1908 Tunguska event: analysis of eyewitness accounts of luminous phenomena collected in 1908*. arXiv.

[53] Brazo, M. W. and Austin, S. A.. (1982). *The Tunguska Explosion of 1908*. Institute for Creation Research.

[54] Earth Science Australia. (1994, June 01). *The 1908 Tunguska Explosion: Atmospheric Disruption of a Stony Meteorite*. Earth Science Australia.

[55] Khrennikov, D.. (2020, October 9). *Tunguska explosion in 1908 caused by asteroid grazing Earth, study suggests.* Astronomy.com.

[56] Phys.org. (2004, August 13). *Tunguska Event: New Details and Sensational Theory.* Phys.org.

[57] Royal Museums Greenwich. (2023, April 06). *The Tunguska Event.* Royal Museums Greenwich.

[58] Tedesco E. F.. (2025, June 23). *Tunguska event.* Encyclopedia Britannica.

[59] Merab, M.. (2023, April 15). *The Tunguska Event: Earth's Brush With APOCALYPSE.* Vocal Media.

[60] Mio, L.. (2001). *The Mad Gasser of Mattoon: You Be the Detective!.* Eastern Illinois University Localities.

[61] American Hauntings. (2023). *The Mad Gasser of Mattoon: Mystery and Mayhem in Weird Illinois.* American Hauntings Ink.

[62] Bartholomew, R. E. & Victor, J. S.. (2004, Spring). *The Mad Gasser of Mattoon.* Wikipedia.

[63] Gargiulo, M.. (2024, March 11). *The Mad Gasser of Mattoon.* Michele Gargiulo.

[64] iHeartPodcasts. (2024, November 28). *LIVE: Minneapolis, The Madd Gasser of Mattoon.* Shortform.

[65] Mattoon in Motion. (2023, October 1). *History and Folklore.* Mattoon in Motion.

[66] Marshall, A.. (2025, January 13). *The Mysterious Mad Gasser of Mattoon (and What We Can Learn From Him).* ExplorersWeb.

[67] D'Mura, C.. (2024, December). *Harvey Wiley and the Pure Food Movement.* Library of Congress Blogs, Inside Adams.

[68] Ashworth, W. B.. (2021, October 8). *Scientist of the Day, Harvey Washington Wiley.* Linda Hall Library.

[69] Reisert, S.. (2019, August 20). *Harvey Wiley's Fierce Pursuit of Food Safety*. Science History Institute.

[70] SmartSense. (2019, September 19). *Heroes of Food Safety: Harvey Wiley, Pioneer and Activist*. SmartSense Blog.

[71] List, G. R.. (2019, July 23). *Harvey W. Wiley (1844-1930)*. AOCS Lipid Library.

[72] EHSO.com. (2025). *Chronology of Food Additive Regulations in the United States*. EHSO.com.

[73] Science Museum Group. (2019, December 01). *Food: A Chemical History*. Science Museum.

[74] Bates, A.. (2019, January 30). *A History of Food Additives*. Fill Your Plate.

[75] Shea T.. (2024, January 9). *Food Additives: What We Eat Today Is NOT What Our Great Grandparents Ate*. FoodNerd Inc.

[76] (n.d.)

[77] Ghost Army Legacy Project. (2023, January 1). *The Inflatable Tank*. Ghost Army Legacy Project.

[78] The National WWII Museum. (2020, February 01). *Ghost Army: The Combat Con Artists of World War II*. The National WWII Museum.

[79] National Veterans Memorial and Museum. (2024, January 15). *The Ghost Army: World War II's Secret Weapon*. National Veterans Memorial and Museum.

[80] Ghost Army Legacy Project. (2024, March 21). *The Ghost Army*. Ghost Army Legacy Project.

[81] Stengle, J.. (2024, March 21). *Ghost Army, masters of WWII deception, awarded Congressional Gold Medal*. Army Times.

[82] Pettersen, M.. (2022, September 20). *Audio Artifacts: When Shure Joined the Allied Forces*. Shure.

[83] Battaglia, A.. (2013, August 14). *The Ghost Army: How Sound Helped Win World War II*. Red Bull Music Academy Daily.

[84] Ouzounian, G.. (2021, July 26). *Powers of Hearing: The Military Science of Sound Location*. The MIT Press Reader.

[85] Recording History. (2015, August 15). *Wire Recorders in World War II*. Recording History.

[86] Hulsey, J. and Trusty, A.. (2018, March 29). *Ellsworth Kelly and the Ghost Army*. Artists Network.

[87] Dudley, M.. (2024, September 14). *Art and the Pacific War*. National Museum of the Pacific War.

[88] Sandstrom, K.. (2024, July 26). *When art went to war: CIA artists in WWII "Ghost Army"*. Cleveland Institute of Art.

Please Consider Leaving a Review

H ELLO THERE!

As an author, I know just how important reviews are for getting the word out about my work. When readers leave a review on Amazon, it helps others discover my book and decide whether it's right for them.

Plus, it gives me valuable feedback on what readers enjoyed and what they didn't.

So if you've read my book and enjoyed it (or even if you didn't!), I would really appreciate it if you took a moment to leave a review on Amazon. It doesn't have to be long or complicated, just a few words about what you thought of the book would be incredibly helpful.

Thank you so much for your support!

Les

Also by

Our catalog is constantly growing!

Visit AdultingHardBooks.com

For our other titles and free bonuses!